Discovering the Book of Common Prayer

A Hands-On Approach

Volume I: Daily Prayer

Sue Careless

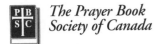 *The Prayer Book
Society of Canada*

 ABC Publishing
ANGLICAN BOOK CENTRE

The Prayer Book Society of Canada
www.prayerbook.ca

ABC Publishing
Anglican Book Centre
600 Jarvis Street, Toronto, Ontario Canada M4Y 2J6
www.abcpublishing.com

All Scripture quotations, unless otherwise indicated,
are taken from the HOLY BIBLE, NEW INTERNATIONAL VERSION ®, NIV®.
Copyright © 1973, 1978, 1984 by International Bible Society.
Used by permission of Zondervan. All rights reserved.

Scripture quotations marked as "RSV" are from
the Revised Standard Version of the Bible, © 1946, 1952, 1971
by the Division of Christian Education
of the National Council of the Churches of Christ in the USA.
Used by permission. All rights reserved.

National Library of Canada Cataloguing in Publication Data

Careless, Sue, 1946–
Discovering the Book of Common Prayer : a hands-on approach / Sue Careless.

ISBN 1-55126-398-X (v. 1)

1. Anglican Church of Canada. Book of Common Prayer. I. Title.

BX5145.5.C37 2003   264'.03   C2003-901969-1

Printed in Canada

Table of Contents

Acknowledgements

The concept for this book first began to take shape in a coffee shop on Bloor Street in Toronto, in April of 2001. Three of us met to exchange ideas about producing a simple user's guide to the Book of Common Prayer: Sue Careless, freelance journalist; Rob Robotham, production manager for the magazine *Faith Today*; and myself, president of the Toronto branch of the Prayer Book Society of Canada. At the time, we were thinking of a modest booklet of about 30 pages, and optimistically estimated that it would be done for Christmas of that year! Nearly two years later, the project has grown and blossomed beyond our wildest expectations.

This book is intrinsically an outgrowth of Sue's vision, enthusiasm, and deep faith. Without her involvement, the project would never have developed as it did. Other people had some hand in making it a success too, however, and we would like to acknowledge their contributions here.

Grateful thanks are due to the members of our review panel, who patiently read through three drafts of the manuscript and made many valuable comments and suggestions: Wilfred Alliston; the Revd. Peter Armstrong; the Revd. Kim Beard; the Revd. Brett Cane; Dorothy Chabot; Dr. William Cooke; Susan Harris; the Revd. Ed Hird; the Revd. Roy Hoult; Bruce Patterson; Dr. Patricia Radcliffe; the Revd. Jeffrey Reed; and the Revd. David Smith. Several others reviewed the manuscript at various stages of its production, and provided much helpful input: Paul Armstrong; Pat Bryan; the Revd. David Burrows; the Rt. Revd. Anthony Burton; the Revd. Darrell Critch; the Revd. Gavin Dunbar; Freya Godard; Dr. Linda Hebb; the Revd. Robert Hudson; the Revd. Charles Irish; Norah Johnston; David Nusko; Larry Rutter; Desmond Scotchmer; and the Revd. Duke Vipperman.

The illustrations and cover art were meticulously produced by David Wysotski of Allure Illustrations. Denyse O'Leary gave the manuscript two careful edits, and Charis Brown-Tobias patiently refined the layout during eight weeks of proofreading. Robert Maclennan of the Anglican Book Centre offered much appreciated technical advice and assistance.

The Prayer Book Society of Canada and its Toronto branch jointly financed this project, and are its proud co-sponsors.

Where not otherwise noted, quotations from the Bible are from the New International Version. Elsewhere they are from the King James Version (indicated as KJV) or from the Revised Standard Version (indicated as RSV). The Book of Common Prayer (1962 Canadian edition) is available from the Anglican Book Centre, 600 Jarvis Street, Toronto, M4Y 2J6 (1-800-268-1168).

We hope that you will enjoy reading this book as much as we enjoyed producing it.

Diana Verseghy
Project Co-ordinator

In the rush to meet frequent deadlines, journalists rarely have time to reflect. So it was a real delight, as well as an honour, to be commissioned by the Prayer Book Society of Canada to ponder prayer and write about it at length.

Writers often joke that there will be no editors in heaven because there writers will be perfect. But here on earth, editors are crucial. I want to thank my first and favourite editor, my husband Tone, who reads everything I write and whose encouragement in writing and in life means everything to me. Editor Denyse O'Leary has long been a respected colleague and close friend of mine, so it was a double pleasure to work with her. The members of the review panel, too, were outstanding in their commitment. Little did they realize the length of the project when they signed on, but they still gave it their full and careful attention. David Wysotski's sensitive art and Charis Brown-Tobias' clean layout have given the text a wonderful lift.

But the person whom I most want to thank is Diana Verseghy. As Project Co-ordinator, she has put in untold hours transforming the Prayer Book Society of Canada's dream into reality. She oversaw and undergirded every aspect of this work. I speak for everyone involved when I thank her for her tireless dedication. What you hold in your hands would not have existed without her.

With God's grace, we Christians are to be a people of joy and prayer. May God use this volume to encourage us all to be more joyful and more prayerful.

Sue Careless

An Introduction by P.D. James

It is both a privilege and a pleasure to write these few words of welcome to this two-volume introductory guide to the Book of Common Prayer published by the Prayer Book Society of Canada. Unhappily the Prayer Book has been neglected both here in the UK and abroad during the past few decades but many in the Church are beginning to rediscover its riches. I hope that these volumes will abundantly succeed in introducing the Prayer Book to thousands of worshippers to whom it may be unknown, and in showing how its use could enrich our spiritual lives.

For over four hundred years Cranmer's Prayer Book has solaced, sustained, rebuked and exalted Christians throughout the English-speaking world, providing for all the rites of passage in this our earthly journey in cadences of incomparable beauty, dignity and grace. For many of us this marvellous book of prayer and praise is part of our early childhood, so that in our private and spontaneous prayers the well-known words of the Book of Common Prayer come readily to our lips and our minds as they do in those moments when we are most in need of God's help, when we see people in distress, when we are touched by compassion, when we experience great moments of joy and exultation for which we need to give thanks. To imagine that people cannot understand the Book of Common Prayer, or that its language is so archaic as to be irrelevant to the twenty-first century, is disproved every day by the millions who love and use it in their corporate and private worship. When we put the Prayer Book into the hands of our children, we do more than introduce them to a priceless part of our religious, cultural and literary heritage; we bestow historic continuity as we pray as our forebears have done for centuries.

I hope that this introductory guide will bring many more Christians and those searching for faith to the treasure of the Prayer Book and will open the eyes of new generations to its riches. Here indeed is language almost worthy of the God it celebrates.

P.D. James
Mystery writer
Patroness of the Prayer Book Society in England

Foreword

I commend this eager and warm-hearted tour guide to the Book of Common Prayer with much enthusiasm and a dash of shame. For, lifelong Anglican though I am, I was very late finding the wisdom of the Prayer Book way.

Seventy years ago, I sat in church Sunday by Sunday for a Prayer Book service that went right over my head. No one explained it, and I did not ask about it; I just daydreamed till it was over.

Sixty years ago, in the days when I thought I was a Christian but wasn't, I watched the grandmother of a friend of mine, an alert old lady born, I think, in the 1860s, go off after breakfast for devotions, holding in her hand the Bible and a large print Book of Common Prayer. What, I wondered, did she do with that Prayer Book? I never asked, so I never found out, though today I think I can guess.

After my conversion, as a callow youth at the University, I was told to pray each morning about that day's living, but none of my Anglican friends ever suggested that the Prayer Book might help me in so doing. Instead, they gave me the idea that pre-set forms for personal prayer were somehow unspiritual, and I believed them.

As a theological student I took an exam on the Prayer Book as a historical document, but how to use it was not part of the syllabus, and was not a matter to which I gave any serious thought.

When I was ordained, half a century ago, I knew I should make personal use of the Prayer Book daily, but I didn't do it. I told myself I would always do better praying out of my head, just as I felt. Was I wrong? Yes.

At last, while teaching in Anglican theological colleges where Prayer Book worship was regularly practised, I began to see that this time-tested compendium of praise and prayer, dating mainly from the sixteenth century, expressed the instincts, needs and desires of my born-again heart in a deeper, wiser, richer and more concentrated way than my own improvisations did, or were likely to do. So my estimate of the Prayer Book went up and up. While I did not stop praying in my own conversational style, chunks of the Prayer Book found their way with increasing frequency into my times with God, and this goes on. It is as if Jesus Christ my Lord, who long ago handed me the Bible so that I might learn his mind, now hands me Prayer Book material to keep me tuned to him and to the Father and the Holy Spirit with him.

Example: I am naturally impatient, but these days, when I have to wait in a line or for a bus or for take-off or for some delayed appointee I brood my way through the *Te Deum*, or some other canticle, or the General Confession and Absolution, or indeed all of Morning Prayer, and my tensions give way to praise, peace, joy and love, and I manage to keep sweet in a way that constantly surprises me. This is one of the many ways in which the Prayer Book does me good.

So, to cut the long story short, I find unique value in our historic Prayer Book, in which the Bible and the gospel are turned into personal and public worship as fruit, fat and flour are turned into cake (something that really can't be said of any of its modern successors); and I want to see it appreciated at its true worth and used still for our growth in grace, that is, for our forward movement, in doxology and devotion.

In saying this, I know, I swim against the stream of the culture of endless novelty, constantly doing things differently and dismissing last year's formula as out-of-date, in which we are all caught up. But C.S. Lewis's admonition against what he called Liturgical

Fidget still surely holds. Worshippers, said Lewis,

> … don't go to church to be entertained. They go to *use* the service, or if you prefer, to *enact* it. Every service is a structure of acts and words through which we receive a sacrament, or repent, or supplicate, or adore. And it enables us to do these things best — if you like, it "works" best — when, through long familiarity, we don't have to think about it. As long as you notice, and have to count, the steps, you are not yet dancing but only learning to dance. A good shoe is a shoe you don't notice. Good reading becomes possible when you need not consciously think about eyes, or light, or print, or spelling. The perfect church service would be one we were almost unaware of; our attention would have been on God.[1]

Why does Sue Careless's survey so delight me? Because it meets us where we are and helps us along this good road. May it find readers worthy of its contents.

J.I. Packer
National Vice-Chairman
Prayer Book Society of Canada

Readers write ...

In empathy with an age that no longer understands its roots, yet grows weary of shallow novelty, Sue Careless lifts the veil, revealing the beauty and depths of the Book of Common Prayer. Readers of varied backgrounds are drawn expertly not simply to understand and appreciate this ancient treasure store, but to join brothers and sisters across time and lands in authentic worship that still surprises by its "uncanny freshness." All this with thoroughness and flair!

Dr. Edith Humphrey
Professor of Scripture and past Dean of
Augustine College, Ottawa

In these uncertain times *Discovering the Book of Common Prayer: A Hands-On Approach* shows the reader what the Book of Common Prayer stands for: a brilliant corporate faith-container, both reformed and catholic, faithful to the faith once delivered, characterized by comprehensible theology and disciplined practice. Sue Careless gives a solid, orthodox and realistic exploration of the Prayer Book, and shows us how faith as expressed in the BCP is for the life participant, not the spectator.

The core message that will be derived from this little volume is a critical reminder for today's Anglican: church life, faith, spirituality, Anglican practice are not about us! They ARE about the living God—Father, Son and Holy Spirit.

The Revd. Dr. Barry Parker
Rector, St. Paul's Church (Bloor St.), Toronto

Sue Careless's guidebook, *Discovering the Book of Common Prayer: A Hands-On Approach,* helps readers connect with the deep roots of Anglicanism. It does so in a clear and refreshing way that renders this rich heritage available to all.

The book helps us to understand the rhythms and the rationale of Anglican worship. Beyond that, the Prayer Book is understood as a beautiful and ordered pathway to an enriched life of personal devotion. Its beauty invites us to a renewed encounter with God. It undergirds the flow of our day and the seasons of our lives.

This is an excellent resource for helping people to become acquainted with the treasure store of our common life as Anglicans.

The Rt. Revd. Ronald Ferris
Bishop of Algoma

Extraordinary Prayers for Everyone

This Book Was Written for You

If you're looking for a richer daily prayer life, if you've been away from the Anglican Church for a long time, or even if you are new to it, this book was written for you.

This is actually a guide to another book—a small, inconspicuous one—that you may not have paid much attention to before.

Does one or more of these situations sound familiar?

▸ You enter an Anglican church and are handed a little burgundy-covered prayer book, or you've found a copy in the pew rack. Perhaps you've never prayed from a book before. Perhaps you've never used "set" or prepared prayers of any kind.

▸ You were confirmed a few years ago, and were given the Book of Common Prayer as a gift. At the time, you felt more excited about the computer games you were given. Perhaps you barely glanced at the book.

▸ You received a white leather copy to carry on your wedding day, along with your bouquet. The flowers wilted long ago, and only now are you beginning to wonder what to make of the Prayer Book.

▸ You have been an Anglican all your life, but your local Anglican church does not use the Book of Common Prayer (BCP) on a regular basis. Or its services are based on the BCP but printed in an edited, bulletin format. You've never really looked inside the book itself.

▸ Your church uses the pew BCP for Morning Prayer and Communion, but you haven't read much else between its covers. You've certainly never considered using the BCP for your private devotions.

You flip through its 700-odd pages and wonder, What are canticles? What is a litany? Absolution? Compline? What days are Maundy Thursday and Whitsunday? Weirdest of all, what are Sexagesima and Quinquagesima? *(See page 45 for the answers.)*

A Priceless Possession of the Anglican Church

This little burgundy-covered book, the Book of Common Prayer (1962 Canadian edition), is the official prayer book of the Anglican Church of Canada. Your pew copy may look rather battered. Yet the BCP is a priceless possession of the Anglican Church and has endeared itself to generations of devout Christians throughout the world. Versions of the Book of Common Prayer are used in over fifty countries and have been translated into over 150 languages. In Canada alone, it is available in French and Inuktitut, Gwich'in, Mohawk, and Cree, as well as English.

Translating the Book of Common Prayer into Aboriginal languages means translating all those unusual words. For example, "Quinquagesima" in Inuktitut is

Ρ ᵇ ᓄ◁ᐋᕐᒪ

Anglicans are not the only ones who pray using the words of the Book of Common Prayer. Over time, other denominations have lifted large chunks out of the BCP, from the marriage and burial rites for example, and put them into their own services. Traditional Lutheran, Methodist and Presbyterian prayer books have all borrowed from the BCP.

This is a guidebook to prayer and the beliefs that underlie the BCP, so we won't go deeply here into its history. If you're curious about where the BCP came from, and why Anglicans first started using it, turn to the Appendix on page 233 for a quick overview of Anglicanism and the BCP from the sixteenth century to the present day.

Becoming More Truly What You Already Are

The Book of Common Prayer, or Prayer Book as it is often called, is held in great affection by all kinds of Anglicans. This is not simply because of its beautiful language (we have only teased you with some of its stranger words), but because it carefully reflects both Holy Scripture and the teaching of the early, undivided Christian Church. The Preface to the Canadian edition states, "This Book of Common Prayer is offered to the Church, with the hope that those who use it may become more truly what they already are: the People of God, that New Creation in Christ which finds its joy in adoration of the Creator and Redeemer of all" *(vii)*. (*Note:* When you see page numbers printed in italics, like the one in the previous line, they refer to pages in the Book of Common Prayer. Page numbers that are not italicized refer to pages in this guide.)

The Prayer Book can help you pray across your lifetime, in part because it spans the centuries. Many of the prayers are ancient biblical ones such as the psalms, some of which are 3,000 years old. Others have been used by generations of worshippers even before the BCP was first compiled in 1549. Prayers that have stood the test of time can still speak with an uncanny freshness today. Over the centuries of the Prayer Book's use, more modern prayers have also been added. The Book of Common Prayer has encouraged countless Christians from a variety of denominations, and can richly expand your prayer life. If you have trouble adoring God, the BCP can help you enormously.

This book is the first of a two-volume series. In this volume we will look at prayer in general and daily prayer in particular, explaining how to incorporate the Prayer Book into your daily devotions. The second volume will focus on the sacraments of **Holy Communion** and **Baptism,** as well as the "occasional" services such as **Holy Matrimony** and the **Ministry to the Sick.**

Not Just for Sundays; Not Just for Priests

Some of the hottest items published are "how-to" books or articles, especially on "how to get organized." We all want to "get it together" or "get a handle" on the messiness of life. We don't want to risk being swamped by the chaos. But we want a pattern that is organic, not mechanistic. The order needs to be life-giving, not soul-destroying.

From its very beginnings, the Book of Common Prayer was designed to be a coherent system (that is, it hangs together), that could provide a firm foundation for one's entire prayer life, either as a cleric or a lay person. It was never intended only for use on Sundays and religious holidays or to mark important milestones in one's life. It was meant to offer a larger pattern of Christian devotion that every worshipper can grow into.

Many people today are familiar only with the passages from the Prayer Book that they hear in church, for example, services of **Holy Communion, Morning Prayer,** and occasional baptisms, weddings, and funerals. But using the BCP only in this limited way misses its inner order and logic.

The broad framework of common prayer according to the BCP invites us to enter into a pattern of daily devotion steeped in Scripture and the regular receiving of the sacraments. The classic pillars of Anglican daily prayer are the BCP's two "Daily Offices" of **Morning** and **Evening Prayer.** In addition to these, however, the BCP surrounds every aspect of life, from the cradle to the grave, from rising to sleep, with Scripture-soaked prayer.

Scripture Arranged for Prayer

Throughout her childhood in Sault Ste. Marie, Ontario, a young woman named Kelly Cooper attended church services that followed the Book of Common Prayer. Only after she was confirmed did she commit herself to reading the Bible regularly. When she did so, her first impression was that the Bible had lifted its text from the Prayer Book, instead of the other way around!

The Book of Common Prayer has been described as "Scripture ordered for prayer" (arranged for prayer). Scholars who have analyzed the text line by line estimate that well over 80 percent of the BCP is taken directly from the Bible. Key passages from the New Testament fill a thick third of the Prayer Book, while the Book of Psalms, the Old Testament's prayer book, fills one quarter. The BCP is soaked in Scripture and, as we shall see, was meant to drench the people who prayed it in Scripture. The Lord's Prayer, which Jesus taught his disciples, is appointed to be said 27 times in the Prayer Book, at least once in every service.

Start at the first page of the Prayer Book, with **Morning Prayer**

(1). See how the first three pages are all verses from Scripture. Now turn to the very last page *(736)* and savour the astonishing blessing of Ephesians 3:20–21.

Most BCP services begin and end with Scripture. The service for the **Burial of the Dead** *(591)* breaks open with a blazing affirmation: "I am the Resurrection and the life, saith the Lord: he that believeth in me, though he were dead, yet he shall live: and whosoever liveth and believeth in me shall never die" (John 11:25–26).

Daily Rhythms and Dramatic Events

The Prayer Book helps us pray biblically, often using prayers straight from the hearts of prophets and psalmists, apostles and martyrs. It helps us pray biblically across the dramatic events of our lifetime (from baptism to burial), but also across the quieter moments of our day from rising to bedtime.

The Prayer Book opens and closes with the rhythms of daily prayer. Both **Morning Prayer** *(1)* and **Evening Prayer** *(17)* are liturgies powerful enough to be celebrated by a large congregation in a cathedral but intimate enough for the private devotions of one soul.

Now flip to the very last page. Turn four leaves in and you are at **Forms of Prayer to be Used in Families** *(728)*. These forms are quite suitable for single people, too. Turn three leaves further in and you'll arrive at **Compline** *(722)*, a hidden jewel. To really appreciate Compline, you need to pray it just before bedtime.

Besides the daily and lifetime rhythms of our prayer life, there is also a weekly rhythm. For the Jew there is the Sabbath and for the Christian, Sunday, when we cease from our labour, from what has been called the tyranny of the urgent, and gather as a faith community for public worship. This rhythm of prayer, too, finds expression in the BCP.

Extraordinary Prayers for Everyone

At first glance, "Book of Common Prayer" seems an unfortunate title. Why would anyone be interested in a book of *common* prayer? If our prayer life is already boring, it can hardly be inspired by a book of common, run-of-the-mill prayers. And, in that sense, the prayers in the BCP do not live down to their billing; they are *un*common. They are often extraordinarily powerful. They pull us out of the valleys and help us ascend the peaks. Some are lovely, even breathtaking, anything but flat and dull. So why are they called "common" prayers?

"Common prayer," in older English, means prayer for all, that is, prayers we all have in common. They belong equally to the whole, worshipping community. They are prayers and services not only for the ordained clergy to say in church, or for nuns and monks to pray in their convents and monasteries, but prayers for the whole people of God. The Book of Common Prayer is for all the faithful who are busy working in the world, whether lab technician or computer analyst, construction worker or sailor, doctor or dancer, parent or child.

Themes and Variations

"We are creatures of habit" yet "variety is the spice of life." Both maxims hold true for those who wish to develop spiritual wisdom. We need regular patterns that offer continuity but we must also avoid getting stuck in a rut. The Prayer Book offers us elements that recur frequently, so their meaning can sink deep down, past merely head knowledge, into our very being. We learn to pray them in our bones. But it also provides a vast array of prayers and psalms, canticles and services over the ever-changing Christian year, so there is always something fresh.

Is God Worth Our Worship? Looking Godward

Dr. J.I. Packer, a world-renowned Anglican scholar, describes *worship* as "ascribing worth to, or acknowledging value in, that which is worshipped." For Christians this means proclaiming "You are worthy" to the Triune God—Father, Son, and Holy Ghost—who is our Creator, Redeemer, and Sanctifier. Dr. Packer continues:

> Worship is looking Godward and celebrating the worth —that is the praiseworthiness—of what we see. The Bible calls this activity glorifying God, or giving glory to God. "Glory" means, first, divinity on display, (the glory God shows us) and then, the responses we make to God for his honour.

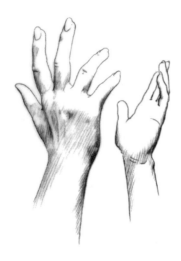

So, after Holy Communion we proclaim

> *Glory* be to God on high, and in earth peace, goodwill towards men. We praise thee, we bless thee, we worship thee, we *glorify* thee, we give thanks to thee for thy great *glory...* (Gloria in Excelsis, 86) [emphasis added]

Dr. Packer also reminds us

> We are constructed so that no activity ever brings us such deep joy as does the worship of God, once we are enabled (through new birth in Christ and through the liberating power of the Holy Spirit) to plunge into it. That is true in this life, and will prove more spectacularly true in the next. God purposes to lead us into more and more of his joy. Worshipping regularly on earth is our training and rehearsal for heaven.[2]

Our Worship Shapes Our Faith

We learn from what we pray. We like to think that our faith shapes our worship and, of course, it does; but it is also true that our worship shapes our faith. The very words we say and the actions we perform as we worship God inform our minds and imaginations, and affect our souls, far more than we realize. So to strengthen our faith we need to strengthen our worship. A Latin maxim, *Lex orandi: lex credendi,* that is, "The law of prayer is the law of belief" sums it up. Anglican scholars have described the Book of Common Prayer as "doctrine in devotion."

If our devotional life is shallow and superficial, and not well-grounded in Scripture, we shouldn't be surprised if we topple in the storms of life. The best worship focuses clearly on God and then brings our world into his presence. We should be careful how we pray.

God's Valentine

**Have you ever thought of the Bible as a love letter?
If not, read on:**

I carried you on eagles' wings and brought you to myself.

(EXODUS 19:4)

I have called you by name, you are mine ...
you are precious in my eyes, and honoured and I love you.

(ISAIAH 43:1B, 4A, RSV)

See, I have engraved you on the palms of my hands.

(ISAIAH 49:16)

I have loved you with an everlasting love.

(JEREMIAH 31:3)

I will betroth you to me forever.

(HOSEA 2:19)

See how the God we are to adore loves us!

Finding the Time; Finding the Words

We need to find the time and the words to enter into dialogue
with this great Lover of our souls. We each have different
amounts of change in our pockets or money in our bank

accounts, but we are all given the same number of hours to spend each day—twenty-four. Yet finding time for prayer is never easy.

Time-management experts tell us that the best way to give ourselves more time is to cut back on television. Four hours of TV per day can add up to ten years of our life!

These same experts also advise us not to cut back on personal time, even when we are under enormous pressure. And Christian prayer is personal time with a personal God. It is time that renews us and helps us refocus. It recharges our batteries. Or, to use another image, we need to find the still point in the dance, the calming peace, before we plunge back into the busyness of life.

Contemporary life does not always allow us to make space for the classic Anglican discipline of praying the Daily Offices (**Morning** and **Evening Prayer**) every day. Yet even if we cannot find the time to undertake the ideal of praying the Daily Offices, we can draw on the many prayer treasures in the BCP that can enrich our prayer life. We will explore these possibilities in this book.

But first, let's look at something that often puzzles newcomers to the Prayer Book—its language.

The Heightened Language of Prayer and the Language of Intimacy

The Book of Common Prayer is considered one of the great works of English literature, along with the King James Version of the Bible and the works of Shakespeare. It was revolutionary in its time because it was written in English, the language of the people. (Prior to its publication, church services had been conducted in Latin.) However, the English used was neither humdrum nor high-flown, but dignified language that both priest and peasant could understand. It is mostly prose, but it has marvellous cadences or rhythms that are crucial to prayer that is shared aloud by a whole congregation. As the language of prayer, it is heightened in intensity but it possesses a clarity and grace that is disarming. It is seldom longwinded. What could be more straightforward than

Minister:	O Lord, open thou our lips;
People:	And our mouth shall show forth thy praise.
Minister:	O God make speed to save us;
People:	O Lord, make haste to help us.

Today we don't use *thou* and *thee*, or *thy* and *thine* in everyday language, but most of us know that *thou* and *thee* mean "you," and *thy* and *thine* mean "your." When the Prayer Book was first written, people used these words in everyday conversation to speak to a close friend or beloved. Such speech suggests intimacy, affection or love. In contrast, *you* and *your* were used to address a person with whom the relationship was more formal or distant.

Of course, no one today uses *thou* to speak to a close friend, so some late twentieth-century revisions of the BCP in other countries have changed *thou* to *you*, arguing in favour of this seemingly less formal approach. In Canada, however, the most recent revision updated some of the archaic language, but still kept the use of *thou*. Many worshippers find it extraordinarily powerful to use a special form of language to address God and fellow members of the Body of Christ. It is a form of language that is now used hardly anywhere else and yet still captures that centuries-old sense of intimacy. Such prayer language can lift us a long way off the ground as we converse with and adore God, and recognize each other as members of his Church.

People Don't Talk Like the Prayer Book!

Obviously, people don't talk like the Prayer Book today. It's not written in the language of the corner store or the coffee shop. Even in Elizabethan England, the Book of Common Prayer was not written in the English of the streets. But its elegant style was grasped and prayed by scholar and ploughman, merchant and milkmaid. Why do we use a more beautiful language when we talk to God? As American David Mills has pointed out in the *Anglican Digest*[3], there are three reasons:

First, *we dress up everything that is important to us.* The teenage boy who lives in his blue jeans rents a tuxedo for his senior prom. The bride carries flowers, even if she is being married at city hall. So Anglicans dress up their communal encounter with the living God in a language of worship that is unusually beautiful.

Second, *we worship with elaborate language because we are talking about God, whom we simply cannot describe in words.* Try to describe your best friend in only ten to twenty-five words. It's not easy, is it? From your verbal description, would a stranger recognize your friend in a crowd?

Speaking about God in words is like trying to draw a circle with straight lines. We cannot do it, but we can come closer to our goal if we use more lines. With three lines we have only a triangle, but with five lines we begin to approach circularity. An octagon is even closer. It is not a circle but it is *like* a circle. As we add more lines, we gradually get close enough to be useful to people who need a picture of a circle.

This is why we often use more complex language when we worship God. We are expressing, as well as humans can, truths beyond words.

Lastly, *this elaborate language is the joyful language of the lover for the beloved.* Think of a girl describing her new boyfriend. She will go on and on, describing every detail of his appearance and personality until her family or friends stop her. Grandparents also cannot say enough about their new grandchild. As lovers, our joy is in the details that we have to speak aloud.

Listen to how the heavenly chorus piles up its adoration:

> Blessing, and glory, and wisdom, and thanksgiving,
> and honour, and power, and might, be unto our God
> for ever and ever.
> (REVELATION 7:12, KJV)

We speak this way to God, not just because we *need* to, to describe him more fully, but because we *want* to, because we love him so dearly.

Not Found in Spell-Checkers

Some verbs in the Prayer Book sound archaic today but their meanings are usually clear, especially when we read them in context:

"Our Father who art in heaven" is "Our Father, [You] who are in heaven." We are talking to God, not about him. Let's look at some of these archaic verbs apart from their context:

art	are
hast	have
showeth	shows
pardoneth	pardons
saith	says

Although the word endings differ from modern usage, the first part of the word, its root, is usually pretty close to the modern version.

Many common English words have also gone through semantic shifts over time. Their spelling hasn't changed, but their meaning has. *Prevent* now usually means "to stop someone from doing something." It originally meant "to anticipate" or "go before" as in:

> Lord, we pray thee that thy grace may always prevent [go before] and follow us, and make us continually be given to all good works; through Jesus Christ our Lord. *Amen.*
> *(244)*

Often, you can see how a change in our language comes about. If you could *prevent* (go before) someone, you might be able to *prevent* (stop) a disaster. In this case, the second usage became the accepted one over time. We'll observe some other words that have changed their meaning as we go along. (*Note:* On page 256

you will find a glossary, where you can check the definitions of many additional words from the BCP.)

Some of the words you do not recognize are not English words at all. They are the traditional Latin titles of canticles or songs of praise such as the *Te Deum* and the *Benedictus*, the *Magnificat* and the *Nunc Dimittis*. Don't worry, the canticles themselves are written in English, and you will pray them in English! You will also notice some new liturgical or worship terms such as *collect, absolution* and *doxology*, and we will explain these as we encounter them.

Truly Inclusive Language

You may be wondering why prayers in the BCP often speak of *men, mankind,* and *brethren*—aren't women included too?

Throughout the twentieth century great strides were made in the establishment of equal social, legal, and political rights for women, leading to the correction of many old injustices. The women and men who brought about these changes challenged areas where men were favoured in ways that resulted in the exclusion or oppression of women. At the same time, though, a mistaken notion grew up that the use of *man* and *mankind* in the older forms of church worship meant that women were excluded from the Church.

But the first writers of the Prayer Book intended the use of *man* and *mankind* as truly inclusive language. Check in any good dictionary: besides the limited definition of "man" as "adult male human being", you will also find the word defined as "human being, as distinct from other animals", and even "the whole human race." *Man* and *mankind* might take a little getting use to, but for centuries they have been used in this broader sense to include every one of us—men, women, and children—made in God's image, parted from him through sin, and redeemed by his mercy through Christ's blood.

Bearing this in mind, it's usually easy to tell from any given passage whether "man" is intended to mean one individual adult male or all of humanity. For example, consider these two excerpts from the service of Holy **Matrimony:**

> The man shall take the ring, and turning to the woman, shall say, "With this ring I thee wed ..." *(566) (Clearly, "man" here means one adult male human being.)*

> Matrimony, which is an honourable estate, instituted of God in the time of man's innocency ... *(564) (Clearly this passage refers to the time of Adam's and Eve's innocence in the Garden of Eden, which is understood as the innocence of all humanity.)*

Hidden Treasures

In this guide we'll focus on daily prayer. However, you will find it useful to navigate the Prayer Book, because there are treasures buried throughout that you'll want to incorporate into your daily devotions. Some of these gems are hidden in unexpected places. For example, look at "A Prayer for Steadfastness" in **Forms of Prayer to be Used at Sea** *(635)*. It is based on a prayer composed by Sir Francis Drake (*c.* 1540–1596), the first Englishman to sail around the world. As a vice-admiral, he also helped defeat the Spanish Armada:

O Lord God, when thou givest thy servants to endeavour any great matter, grant us also to know that it is not the beginning but the continuing of the same until it be thoroughly finished, which yieldeth the true glory; through him that for the finishing of thy work laid down his life, our Redeemer, Jesus Christ. *Amen.*

(635)

The service at sea contains several other marvellous prayers we can use on land, including one for those who travel and this one for loved ones far away:

O God, who art present in every place: Look down with thy mercy upon those whom we love, now absent from us; give thine angels charge over them, and defend them from all dangers of body and soul; bring us together again, if it be thy holy will; grant that both they and we, drawing nearer to thee, may draw nearer to one another, and in the end, united in thy presence, may evermore rejoice together in our heavenly home; through Jesus Christ our Lord. *Amen.*

(633)

And here is one for a weary soul:

> O Lord, support us all the day long of this troublous [trouble-filled] life, until the shadows lengthen and the evening comes, the busy world is hushed, the fever of life is over and our work is done. Then, Lord, in thy mercy, grant us safe lodging, a holy rest, and peace at the last; through Jesus Christ our Lord. *Amen.*
>
> *(58, 634)*

If you need a prayer "For Freedom from Worry" (and who doesn't need that?) check under **Family Prayers at Evening** *(730)*.

At Your Fingertips: A Hands-On Approach

So let's begin with an overview. You could read the table of contents *(v)*, but let's take a more "hands-on" approach and simply open the Prayer Book near the middle *(page 331)*. You are at the beginning of the Psalter (pronounced "Salter"). These psalms fill the third quarter of the Prayer Book.

Now divide the first half of the book into quarters. The second quarter will fall open somewhere in the section called "The Christian Year," which contains the Collects, Epistles, and Gospels for different Sunday services of **Holy Communion.** That section comes right after the service of **Holy Communion** itself. This is a rough rule of thumb, but it will help you find your way faster than some seasoned Anglicans!

Special Occasions

a. The human life cycle from birth to death

Now try opening the book again to the centre and then to the last quarter. You should be close to one of four **baptism** services *(522–543)*, perhaps the one for those of "riper years" *(532)*. This title sounds a bit eccentric, but it means just what it says, baptism for those who are older than a young child. You are now in the "occasional" services, meaning services for special occasions. These services of **Baptism, Confirmation, Matrimony, Thanksgiving After Childbirth, Ministry to the Sick,** and **Burial of the Dead** follow the human life cycle (birth, youth, marriage, sickness, death), not the rhythms of daily life (morning, mid-day, and evening) that open and close the Prayer Book. This section also contains material on what Anglicans believe, such as the **Catechism** *(544)*, which is traditionally studied by Anglicans before they are confirmed and publicly proclaim their faith.

b. Miscellaneous services for penance and harvest, students and sailors

Next come four occasional but unrelated services for special situations: **A Penitential Service** *(611)*, to be used on Ash

Wednesday (the first day of Lent, a season stressing repentance) and at other times that demand profound repentance; **Thanksgiving for the Blessings of Harvest** *(617)*; **A Service for Young People** *(622)*; and **Forms of Prayer to be Used at Sea** *(628)*. We can find ourselves in many different places in life but in any circumstance, the Prayer Book helps us approach God.

c. Occasions in the life of the church

Next we have services that focus on the clergy (the ordination of deacons and priests, and the consecration of bishops) *(637–667)* and services for the life cycle of a parish, such as the induction of a rector and the blessing of church buildings and properties *(668–694)*.

d. Doctrine and history

If you want to understand what Anglicans have traditionally believed, start first with the second-century Apostles' Creed *(10)* and the fourth-century Nicene Creed *(71)*. Then read the **Catechism** *(544)*. If you want to go deeper, then turn to this section *(695–721)*. Here you will find the third historic Christian creed, **The Creed of Saint Athanasius** (commonly so called) *(695)* which stresses particularly the Trinity and the Incarnation. It was probably composed after AD 428. Next come the **Articles of Religion** *(698)*, or the **Thirty-Nine Articles,** as they are usually called. These teachings were written at the time of the Reformation to set out the Anglican position on various issues that were raised and debated during that period. They were finalized in 1571. Finally, you can read the **Original Preface** to the Book of Common Prayer (1549) altered in 1552 and 1662 *(715)*. (You may need a magnifying glass for the fine print!)

The Book of Common Prayer at a Glance

First quarter:
- ▶ Daily Offices of Morning, Mid-day, and Evening Prayer
- ▶ Additional Canticles (for Morning and Evening Prayer)
- ▶ The Litany
- ▶ Prayers and Thanksgivings
- ▶ A Bidding Prayer
- ▶ The Lord's Supper or Holy Communion

Second quarter: *Collects, Epistles, and Gospels for Sunday services of Holy Communion throughout the year*

Third quarter: *The Psalter (psalms)*

Fourth quarter: *Occasional Services*
- ▶ Baptism of Children
- ▶ Baptism of Adults
- ▶ Private [emergency] Baptism
- ▶ Public Receiving of Those Privately Baptized
- ▶ The Catechism
- ▶ Confirmation
- ▶ Matrimony
- ▶ Thanksgiving after Childbirth
- ▶ Ministry to the Sick
- ▶ Burial of the Dead *(cont'd on page 44)*

The Book of Common Prayer at a Glance *(cont'd)*

Occasional Services *(cont'd)*
- ▶ A Penitential Service
- ▶ Harvest Thanksgiving
- ▶ Service for Young People
- ▶ Prayers to be Used At Sea

Occasional Services for clergy and parish life
- ▶ Ordination or consecration of clergy: deacons, priests and bishops
- ▶ Induction (of a rector)
- ▶ Laying foundation stone of church or chapel
- ▶ Consecration of church or chapel
- ▶ Consecration of graveyard

Doctrine and history *(see also Catechism & Apostles' and Nicene Creeds)*
- ▶ Creed of St. Athanasius
- ▶ Articles of Religion
- ▶ Historical Prefaces

More daily prayers *(ideal for private use)*
- ▶ Compline
- ▶ Family Prayer

And the answer is ...

(Answers to the questions on page 22)

1. A canticle is a hymn or song of praise, usually found in the Bible but not typically from the Book of Psalms.

2. A litany is a series of petitions read by a prayer leader to which the congregation makes short, set responses.

3. Absolution is a declaration of forgiveness pronounced in God's name by a priest after confession.

4. Compline is a short service said just before bedtime. Such forms of prayer date back to the Middle Ages.

5. Maundy Thursday is the Thursday before Easter, when Jesus washed the disciples' feet at the Last Supper and gave them a new commandment, "that you love one another as I have loved you" (John 13:34). "Maundy" comes from the Latin word for "commandment", *mandatum*, which became *mandé* in Old French, and then *maundy* in Middle English.

6. Whitsunday is the traditional English name for the feast of Pentecost, marking the coming of the Holy Spirit to enliven the church.

7. Sexagesima is Latin for "sixtieth" and means the eighth Sunday before Easter (approximately the sixtieth day). Easter is the great feast of the Christian year, so a countdown of sorts is observed.

8. Quinquagesima is Latin for "fiftieth," and means the seventh Sunday before Easter (approximately the fiftieth day).

Exploring Prayer in General

> I only pray when I am in trouble. But I am in trouble all
> the time, and so I pray all the time.[4]
> – *Isaac Bashevis Singer, Nobel Prize-winning author*

Christian prayer has been described as an act of true helplessness
in which we come closest to reality, recognizing God's greatness
and our own weakness. We live in a fallen world that, like
ourselves, is troubled by sin. So there is always lots to pray about.

American novelist Anne Lamott writes that the two best prayers
she knows are, "Help me! Help me! Help me!" and "Thank you!
Thank you! Thank you!" Lamott certainly hasn't covered all the
elements of worship in her two simple prayers, but she has struck
two key chords. She acknowledges her dependency on God and
her gratefulness to him.[5]

As we said earlier, this first volume in the series *Discovering the
Book of Common Prayer: A Hands-On Approach* tells how you can
use the BCP in your daily prayers. But first we need to talk
about prayer itself. Many of us have trouble entering into prayer
on our own. Let's look at various ways to approach prayer and

hence, to approach God, remembering, paradoxically, that he first approaches us.

Gossiping about God

Many of us love to talk *about* God, but spend precious little time actually talking *with* him. It is as though we gossip behind God's back but fail to talk to him face to face. And when we do pray, we don't enter into a dialogue with God; we rattle on in a monologue, or we become tongue-tied.

The disciples asked Jesus, "Lord, teach us to pray." Notice, they didn't ask, "Lord, teach us to preach, evangelize, and perform miracles." Their request is itself a prayer, and it was answered. We all need to learn how to pray across the day and across our lives.

Prayer Is...

To *pray* comes from the Latin word, *precare*, meaning "to beg" or "to entreat." The noun *prayer* is thought to come from a late Latin noun *precaria*, meaning "entreaty." There are many ways of describing the mystery of prayer. Here are a few:

▶ Prayer is the raising of the mind and heart to God.

▶ Prayer is yearning for God, homesickness for God.

▶ Prayer is exposing ourselves honestly to God in intimate conversation.

▶ Prayer is intentionally placing oneself in God's presence and waiting upon him.

▶ Prayer seeks the union of our will with God's will.

▶ Prayer sustains the friendship we have with a personal God.

▶ In prayer we enter into a transforming relationship with God. We come away changed.

(For more descriptions of prayer turn to page 230.)

Under God's Gaze

In prayer we come to God to know him and to open ourselves up to him. We may understand in our heads that we are at all times perfectly known by God, but we want to encounter him, to enter into his presence. Although he may seem absent to our minds or senses, he is, in fact, always present to those who humbly approach him. God is "always more ready to hear than we to pray" (Collect for the 12th Sunday after Trinity, *page 236*). In the service called **Compline,** we repeat the words of the prophet Jeremiah, "Thou, O Lord, art in the midst of us and we are called by thy name. Leave us not, O Lord our God" (Jeremiah 14:9).

Am I Just Talking to Myself?

The French Roman Catholic bishop, Francis de Sales (1567–1622), said that the first step in meditation and prayer is "to place oneself in the presence of God." But this is not always as easy as it sounds. We need to be clear about who God is and where he is to be found. And there is another problem. Who is the "real" me that I am placing in his presence? Anglican author C.S. Lewis wrote, "In prayer this real I struggles to speak, for once, from his real being… The prayer preceding all prayers is, 'May it be the real I who speaks. May it be the real Thou that I speak to.'"[6]

Do We Pray to the "god within us?"

> Am I only a God nearby and not a God far away?
> (JEREMIAH 23:23)

Some people today talk about praying to the "god within." Some will even say they don't believe in any god outside of themselves,

that God only exists within people. They have given up on a transcendent God who exists beyond themselves. They only acknowledge an immanent god, a god within.

Is this what the Bible teaches? Do Christians only pray to a god within, to our own souls, as it were? Is prayer only self speaking to self?

As Christians, we believe in a transcendent, holy God who exists independently of us. He is eternally real whether we acknowledge him or not, whether we experience his presence or not. He does not come into existence when we acknowledge him and evaporate when we don't. We don't create this holy God in our own image. How could we, for we are sinners, albeit sinners saved? (Although we are clever at conjuring up false gods who are far more comfortable to live with.)

God has an independent reality which, by his grace, we may gradually come to know personally. He graciously reveals his holy self to us human beings, and that is why we speak of God's revelation. He reveals something of himself in his natural world, his creation. This is called *general revelation*. But we see God most clearly in the face of Jesus. And we see Jesus best in Scripture, or *special revelation*, as theologians call it.

When we accept Christ as our Lord and Saviour, he comes to live within our souls and bodies by the power of his Holy Spirit which transforms (sanctifies) us. Our bodies become his holy temple:

> Do you not know that your body is a temple of the Holy Spirit, who is in you, whom you have received from God? You are not your own. You were bought at a price. Therefore honour God with your body.
>
> (1 CORINTHIANS, 6:19–20)

Another Lives in Me

St. Ignatius of Antioch (*c*.35–*c*.107) said on the way to his death as a martyr, "Another is in me."

St. Paul said, "I have been crucified with Christ and I no longer live but *Christ lives in me*. The life I live in the body, I live by faith in the Son of God, who loved me and gave himself for me" (Galatians 2:20). St. Paul also spoke of "the glorious riches of this mystery, which is *Christ in you*, the hope of glory" (Colossians 1:27). *[emphasis added in quotations above]*

So our God is both *transcendent* (beyond us) and *immanent* (close within us). He is not a manifestation of ourselves, a projection of our spiritual imagination or a group hallucination the Church is having. He is always an objective Other. We don't mystically merge. We do not pray to "the god in us," but we look up and out and beyond ourselves as we worship, and sometimes, then, sense him drawing near.

If, however, we navel-gaze, if we don't raise our spiritual vision beyond ourselves, we will never be caught up in him. Our spiritual universe needs to be bigger than our own tiny, egotistical world, and when it is, God paradoxically enters even into our own corner of reality and deepens it immeasurably.

The night he was betrayed, Jesus prayed for us to his Father, saying,

> Righteous Father, … I have made you known to them [those you have given me], and will continue to make you known in order that the love you have for me may be in them and that *I myself may be in them.*
> (JOHN 17:25–26) *[emphasis added]*

In the beautiful prayer just before Communion, we ask that the sacrament may help us stay in this relationship with God, "that we may evermore dwell in him [Christ], And he in us." *(84)*

We are not worshipping ourselves when we worship Christ. Another lives in us. We can know his presence; but we are two separate identities that, by his grace, in his Spirit, have an intimate relationship.

Do We Worship Nature?

We all need to open our senses more to the wonders of nature in all its "vast array" (Genesis 2:1). You may draw the line at sensing skunks and mosquitoes. Yet even the common housefly is breathtaking under a microscope. John Calvin called creation the "theatre of God's glory." Today we exclaim, "Awesome!"

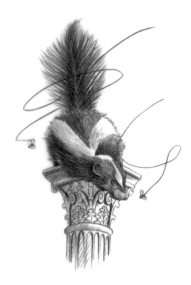

But we should never worship the creature instead of the Creator. Just as we are not to worship ourselves, even though we are made in the image of God, so we are not to worship anything else God has created, even though it reflects something of his magnificent glory:

> The heavens declare the glory of the Lord; and the firmament showeth his handiwork.
>
> (PSALM 19:1) *(351)*

Creation helps stretch our vision of God. The moon shining in the sky reflects something of the sun; yet the moon is not the sun. So the sun reflects something of God's glory but is not God. God is more than us and he is more than all his creation. To say so diminishes neither man nor nature. We need to respect, not exploit, human beings, because they are made in the image of God. So we speak of the sanctity of human life. And we need to respect, not exploit, his glorious creation.

Do you remember the first four words in the Bible?

"In the beginning God…" Stop there. God existed before the world and apart from the world. Now let's read the whole verse: "In the beginning God created the heavens and the earth" (Genesis 1:1).

So we learn that God existed before he created the heavens and the earth, and that he created them out of nothing.

Holy Tension

Christians worship a God larger than the amazingly intricate cosmos, yet a God who entered into that cosmos, an infinite God who entered world history and by his Holy Spirit draws near to us. We worship an intimate, incarnational Christ who entered into our human flesh, yet sinned not, who entered into creation, yet rules over it. We need to maintain this holy tension of awe and intimacy in our worship.

The psalms speak of the creation worshipping its Maker and of the Creator caring for his creation. If you enjoy nature, you will love praying these psalms: 8, 18, 19, 29, 104, and 148. God is the Lord of (over) Creation. **Morning** and **Evening Prayer** issue these biblical invitations to worship *(3, 17):*

O worship the Lord in the beauty of *holiness*: let the whole earth stand in awe of him.
(PSALM 96:9)

The Lord is in his *holy* temple: let all the earth keep silence before him.
(HABAKKUK 2:20)

Thus saith the high and lofty One that inhabiteth eternity, whose name is *Holy:* I dwell in the high and *holy* place, with him also that is of a contrite and humble spirit.

(ISAIAH 57:15) *[emphasis added]*

So humans, along with the whole of creation, are to worship their Creator. He is not only larger and infinitely wiser than the creation he made; he is, as these verses remind us, holier. The Old Testament's hymn book, the Psalter, closes with this verse: "Let everything that hath breath praise the Lord" (Psalm 150:6).

False Choices

Decisions about prayer don't have to be "either/or," though we sometimes make them as if they were. Often, the answer can be "both."

Try this quiz:

Should we pray in solitude or in the midst of the marketplace?
Should we practise activism or contemplation?
Should we pray set or spontaneous prayers?
Should we establish a prayer routine with definite rhythms, or should we be innovative?
Should we only pray in real emergencies and on special occasions, or during each day?

Answer: *All of the above.*

You don't have to choose between activism and contemplation. Drawing apart to be with God can help us engage better with the world around us. Liturgical or set prayer can prime the soul for spontaneous prayer.

Closet, Car Pool, and Congregation

We need to pray in solitude, quietly alone—although, as we shall see, we are never spiritually alone. Jesus told us, "When you pray, go into your room, close the door and pray to your Father who is unseen. Then your Father, who sees what is done in secret will reward you" (Matthew 6:6). We may not always have a private room available. Jesus himself went out to a mountain or garden or wilderness (Mark 1:35). But we enter into an inner space. We also need to pray amidst the clamour of the world, in the fast lane of life. And we need to pray corporately in the congregation, gathered in the assembly of God's people. In each location, the worship styles will be very different, but they are all legitimate places of prayer.

It's Not All Up to You

Prayer is a gift from God, a grace. It's a gift he gives us, so we can offer it back to him. Christian prayer is based on our relationship with God. But just as he initiates the friendship, so he initiates the prayerful conversation. He sparks the desire to dialogue and he helps us sustain it.

I Can't Do This Alone!

We can easily feel very alone when we pray. Yet we are never, ever alone. We need to remember that God in his three persons is spiritually present with us, not only listening to us, but even praying for us and through us. This is the Trinitarian model of prayer.

Christians pray to the Father, through the Son, by the inspiration of the Holy Spirit. Here's how C.S. Lewis explained it in *Mere Christianity:*

> An ordinary simple Christian kneels down to say his prayers. He is trying to get into touch with God. But if he is a Christian, he knows that what is prompting him to pray is also God: God, so to speak, inside him. But he also knows that all his real knowledge of God comes through Christ, the Man who was God—that Christ is standing beside him, helping him to pray, praying for him. You see what is happening. God is the thing to which he is praying—the goal he is trying to reach. God is also the thing inside him which is pushing him on— the motive power. God is also the road or bridge along which he is being pushed to that goal. So that the whole threefold life of the three-personal Being is actually going on in that ordinary little bedroom where

an ordinary man is saying his prayers. The man is being caught up into the… spiritual life: he is being pulled into God, by God, while still remaining himself.[7]

When we Christians pray on earth, we do so by the inspiration of the indwelling Holy Spirit, who is encouraging us to pray and interpreting even our sighs and groans to the Father, who listens attentively. Meanwhile, in heaven, Jesus is also speaking on our behalf to the Father.

The Trinity, one God in three persons, may be a hard concept for theologians to make clear, but when it comes to prayer it is a totally awesome and encouraging model that Scripture fully supports. Let's unpack it a bit more.

To God and through God

We pray *to the Father* who listens:

Before they call, I will answer,
While they are still speaking, I will hear.

(ISAIAH 65:24)

Jesus reassures us, "Your Father knows what you need before you ask him."

(MATTHEW 6:8)

We pray *through the Son*, who is the great High Priest. In the Old Testament the high priest spoke to God on behalf of the Israelites. He prayed for them to God:

(cont'd on page 60)

To God and through God (cont'd)

> Seeing then that we have a great high priest that is passed into the heavens, Jesus the Son of God, ... let us therefore come boldly unto the throne of grace, that we may obtain mercy and find grace to help in time of need.
>
> (HEBREWS 4:14–16, KJV)

And *the Son prays* for us:

> Jesus, our great high priest, is able to save completely all who come to God through him, because he always lives to intercede for them.
>
> (HEBREWS 7:25)

We pray by the *inspiration of the Holy Spirit:*

> In the same way, the Spirit helps us in our weakness. We do not know what we ought to pray for, but the Spirit himself intercedes for us with groans that words cannot express. And he [God the Father] who searches our hearts knows the mind of the Spirit, because the Spirit intercedes for the saints in accordance with God's will.
>
> (ROMANS 8:26, 27)

These beautiful passages on prayer assure us that prayer is not all verbal head-knowledge and logic. There is a certain mystery to prayer, just as there is a mystery to God. The prayers of two-year-olds and mentally challenged adults, of geniuses and those suffering from dementia, will all be heard by God the Father because of the inspiration of his indwelling Holy Spirit. Jesus said, "Out of the mouth of babes and sucklings thou hast brought perfect praise" (Matthew 21:16, RSV).

We are "the saints" the Holy Spirit encourages, if we have
entrusted our lives to God. When we are in our small room or
tiny church, we may feel as though any prayer we utter will just
bounce off the ceiling and fall to the floor. Not so. It is as
though the ceiling opens and God on his heavenly throne is
bending down, hearing our every word. In fact, he is listening
before we even open our mouths or our hearts to him. The
psalmist says:

> All my longings lie open before you, O Lord,
> my sighing is not hidden from you.
>
> (PSALM 38:9)

Dirty Laundry

We need to recognize, however, that we cannot approach God in
our own righteousness, having done our own laundry. For in the
brilliant light of his holiness, "all our righteous acts are like filthy
rags" (Isaiah 64:6). We need to bring the soiled garments of our
lives to him. Only he can cleanse us and make us truly holy.

In Revelation 19:8, the Church, the bride of Christ, is given "fine linen, bright and clean," to wear. And St. Paul urges us to "clothe ourselves with the Lord Jesus Christ" (Romans 13:14) and "put on Christ" (Galatians 3:27, KJV). Jesus is our holy garment of righteousness.

Through the Gates of Repentance

To change the metaphor, we need to come humbly through the gates of repentance. We should pray honestly and sincerely. Jesus is our sinless, great High Priest and also our Sacrifice. He is our Saviour through whom we receive forgiveness and grace. Because of him we can confidently approach the throne of grace. The Holy Spirit understands our weakness and strengthens us to come before the presence of God. So, with the help of the whole Trinity, our prayers pierce heaven and are enfolded in the Father's heart.

Name-Dropping

Now, notice how almost all Christian prayers seem to close with some mention of Jesus such as "through Jesus Christ our Lord" or "through our Lord and Saviour Jesus Christ." Christians usually pray to the Father through the Son by the power of the Holy Spirit.

In settings of interfaith worship, where there are representatives from various faiths offering prayer, some people wish to mention only "God" or "God the Father" or "Lord," so that no offence is given to those who don't embrace Jesus.

But Christians believe that we cannot approach so holy a God in our own shabby goodness; we just don't measure up. It actually shows great humility and honesty to admit that only through trusting Jesus can we approach God; only through Jesus' blood shed on the cross is God our spiritual Father.

But wait. Aren't we all God's children? Didn't he create us all? Yes, but St. Paul tells us, "all have sinned and fall short of the glory of God" (Romans 3:23). Christians call God "Father" now by adoption. We have been adopted into his family through faith or trust in Jesus, the only natural Son, who was obedient unto death.

We Never Pray Alone—Ever!

So the whole Trinity is supporting you as you pray. You pray in the company of the Trinity.

But there is more. No one is meant to be a solitary Christian. Even in the extreme isolation of solitary confinement, a Christian prays, not only with the Trinity and through the Trinity, but also with the whole household of faith here on earth. This church on earth is called the church militant. It consists of the body of Christians still alive in this world, "militant" because their battle with evil is not yet over.

The prayer Jesus taught us begins, "Our Father," not "My Father." We are baptized into a family. We become God's children at baptism but we also gain brothers and sisters in the faith. We don't come before God as isolated individuals, not even in our private devotions, but as members of a family, a community of faith, the communion of saints. And as we pray, they too are praying around the globe, in Ghana, Germany, and Guatemala. We have a Father in this often fatherless world, but we also have siblings. We need to remember they are praying with us and for us, worshipping our common Father. This is the community of the redeemed, sinners forgiven but still alive on earth.

So the three persons of the Trinity support us as we pray, and the church militant throughout all the earth prays with us. But there is still more.

The Church Triumphant

Whenever we pray, no matter how feebly, we are joining the mighty heavenly chorus in adoration. The saints and martyrs who have entered heaven compose the church triumphant and along with the angels shout, "Holy, holy, holy!" So next time you feel all alone, or your congregation is pathetically small, remember that you are not alone at all. We pray spiritually with the whole Body of Christ, his church militant here on earth and his church triumphant in heaven. We will see later how the *Te Deum*, **Morning Prayer's** glorious ancient hymn, underscores this *(7)*.

Creation Crowds In

Now if that is not enough, creation itself praises God. "The heavens declare the glory of the Lord and the firmament showeth his handiwork" (Psalm 19:1) *(351)*. In Psalm 148, as well as in the canticle *Benedicite (26)*, ice and snow, seas and floods, beasts and cattle are all urged to praise and magnify God. So if you open your eyes of faith, you'll see there is quite a crowd worshipping God with you. Only the devil wants you to feel abandoned.

Many-Faceted Gem

The gemstone of prayer has many facets, and we should become familiar with all of them. Otherwise our prayer conversation soon loses depth and becomes a boring monotone. Even a small child can grasp the main types of prayer: "the praises" (adoration), "the thank-yous" (thanksgiving), "the sorrys" (confession), "the pleases" (personal petition and intercession), and "the blesses" (blessings).

We fail at good diet and exercise programs because we do not build enough variety into them. How long can anyone eat only grapefruit for breakfast? If you want your low-fat diet to succeed, keep plenty of different low-fat foods on hand. If you are embarking on an exercise program, make sure it is well-balanced. All weight-bearing and no stretching or flexing will be not only dull but harmful. You will only stick with programs that have a rich variety to them. We need plenty of diversity in our prayer life as well; otherwise we will quickly abandon it.

"Please" or "Help!" in prayer is called petition, request, or *supplication*. Asking help for someone else is *intercession*. "Thank you!" of course is *thanksgiving*. It has been said that an atheist is someone who has no one to thank. Remember how lousy or vaguely unsatisfying it feels to open gifts with no one around to thank? Expressing gratitude to the giver actually increases our delight in the gift.

Alphabet Soup

You should try to structure your prayer life to include what is best remembered under the acronym, ACTS: adoration, confession and commitment (or consecration), thanksgiving, and supplication. Some prefer the acronym PRAY: praise, repentance, asking, and yielding, which is surrender or commitment to God. We'll see how the Prayer Book ensures that you "cover all the bases."

An acronym to help your prayer life

A adoration
C confession and commitment (or consecration)
T thanksgiving
S supplication

Another useful acronym

P praise
R repentance
A asking
Y yielding (surrender or commitment to God)

You might also find it helpful to remember these types of prayer under the four Gs. In prayer we

▸ Praise God for his **G**lory
▸ Confess to him our **G**uilt
▸ Thank him for his **G**oodness
▸ Ask for his **G**race

We ask for his enabling grace both for ourselves and for others. Some people find it helpful to think of prayer in terms of time as well: past, present, and future. This model doesn't cover all the aspects of prayer, but it is still helpful.

In the Lord's Prayer we ask for

▸ **P**ardon from the past
▸ **P**rovision for the present
▸ **P**rotection for the future

But enough of this alphabet soup. Let's explore some of these aspects of prayer in more depth.

Adoration: Madly in Love

Adoration actually means "worship," from the Latin, *adorare*, "to speak or pray towards." Besides "to worship or offer reverence to as divine," to *adore* also means "to regard with honour and deep affection."

When you romantically adore someone, you want to be continually in that person's presence to catch his or her every look and word. When you have to be away, you try to recall all you can about your beloved. When you adore someone, you certainly don't ignore or forget that person. Instead, you are often so wrapped up in the one adored that you actually forget about yourself!

Adoration of God lifts us up out of ourselves and into God's presence. We forget about ourselves and hang on his every word. If we neglect adoration, our perception of God can shrink to an afterthought. Praising God does not make him bigger than he actually is, but in glorifying him our understanding stretches. We will never totally comprehend God, but as we look towards him in praise, we see more of his true nature.

adore:	praise, glorify, magnify, honour
magnify thy holy name:	make God's name and reputation to be more openly known and praised

Is God Vain?

Why does God need all this praise? Aren't Christians supposed to be humble and not boast? St. Paul said he would only boast about God, and that was not boasting in the sense of exaggerating but of telling the real truth about God. We need this sense of who God really is. God doesn't. He has a clear sense of his identity. Just as we thank human benefactors for their kindnesses towards us, so we thank our God. It is a powerful way to remind ourselves of his goodness towards us. Both in worship and out in the world, we should speak openly about our God and less about ourselves. When we marginalize God, we short-change everyone.

Lukewarm Love

Now, adoration is the high point of worship, when we come closest to a sense of God's holy presence. But some days this can also be the hardest, even the most boring part of worship. Why? Because we are still so caught up in ourselves.

We have lost our "first love" for God, as Jesus accused the church at Ephesus. We are only "lukewarm" in our affections, as he charged the church at Laodicea (Revelation 2, 3). What would he say to our congregation? We may have little desire to honour God with praise; yet as we do, some of that love is rekindled.

We are eager to talk to God about our needs and our concerns for others. God certainly wants to hear these petitions. We will actually have more confidence in making these requests if we have already reminded ourselves that our God is a big God who can handle huge needs. If we have only a trivial god, then why bother asking him for anything? He won't be able to deliver. So praising God first will actually give us the confidence to petition him boldly later. We'll see in Chapter Four how in both **Morning** and **Evening Prayer**, we praise God first before we petition him. We reverence him and then we make our requests.

Boooooring!

We love to receive praise and we like hearing our friends applauded, although we can get jealous. We're not interested, however, in hearing high praise for a stranger. It can be tiresome hearing people go on at great length about someone they admire whom we have never met. We might become curious about meeting this person, or we might just switch off. It can get pretty boring if you don't know the person being praised.

Some of us may never have had a "first love" for God, only a nominal faith that has insulated us from the real thing. If we don't personally know God and are not personally committed to God, then all this high praise and glorious talk about him can be tedious. Or we might get caught up in it and want to meet this amazing person for ourselves. He reveals himself to us as we praise him. After all, he dwells in the praises of his people (Psalm 22:3).

Get Real!

We need to tell God the truth. "God, you are not real to me. This praise stuff is all unreal to me. Please, if you are real, Jesus, make yourself known to me in the praises of your people, so I can worship you, too, and really mean it."

Locating Prayers of Adoration

Songs of adoration flood the Psalter. Read Psalms 47, 66, 84, 96–98, 103, 104, 113, 145–150. Moses, Miriam, and Hannah also offer up glorious songs of praise which we can echo (Exodus 15:1–21 and 1 Samuel 2). David bursts into praise and thanksgiving to the Lord in 1 Chronicles 29:10b–14.

Then there is the hymn book of heaven. Without a doubt, Revelation, the last book of the Bible, is also the most difficult to grasp, but its praise, the worship of heaven, is a must read (pray, sing) for every Christian. Almost all the verse sections are praise. You might want to read them all at one go: Revelation:1:6b–8; 4:8–11; 5:9–14; 7:9–17; 11:15–19; 12:7–12; 15:3b–4; 16:5–7; 19:1–9; 21:1–7; 22:2–21. "Amen. Come, Lord Jesus."

The Prayer Book is brimming with canticles, which are songs of praise. As we said earlier, they are called by their traditional Latin names: *Venite (6), Te Deum (7), Benedictus (9), Magnificat (21), Nunc Dimittis (22), Benedicite, Omnia Opera (26), Cantate Domino (28), Surge, Illuminare (28)* and *Jubilate Deo (457).* We will look more closely at each of these bursts of praise in Chapter Four. Holy Communion has a glorious piece of adoration that is said or sung by the people after they have received communion, but it can also be used in private devotions. It begins with the song of the angels to the shepherds: "Glory be to God on high," in Latin, *Gloria in Excelsis (86).*

There are also special anthems said or sung on Christmas Day *(104)*, Good Friday *(173)*, Easter *(182)*, and Pentecost *(204)* that take the place of the *Venite.* Each anthem is a powerful compilation of Scripture verses. The anthem for Good Friday closes with the song of the heavenly host in Revelation: "Worthy is the Lamb that was slain to receive power, and riches, and wisdom, and strength, and honour, and glory, and blessing" (Revelation 5:12).

Confession: The Lost Son

Jesus told many stories or parables. One of the best loved is the story of the lost son. A young man demands that his father pay him his inheritance, which he does. The son takes the money and goes to a far country, where he wastes every coin. Finally he finds himself reduced to tending pigs, so hungry that he chews their corn. You can read the whole story in Luke 15:11–31.

The son decides to return home. "I will arise and go to my father and say unto him, 'Father, I have sinned against heaven and before thee and am no more worthy to be called thy son…'" (Luke 15:18–19, KJV). We sometimes hear these words at the opening of **Morning** and **Evening Prayer** *(pages 3* and *18)*. The son recognizes his sinfulness and returns to his father in the hope of being taken back, not as a son embraced by his family, but as a hired servant kept at a distance.

Meanwhile, his father had been watching every day for his return. When he saw his child "a long way off," the father "was filled with compassion for him; he ran to his son, threw his arms around him and kissed him" before the child could say a word! Then the son repeats the very words he decided upon in the pigpen.

Now the father in the parable doesn't deny the sinfulness of his son by saying "Oh, no, my child. You did nothing terribly wrong." Nor is he a taskmaster exacting payment: "You will have to work for me for *x* number of years, and then I'll think about accepting you back into the family." No. To celebrate his son's return he calls for a feast—delectable fare after pigs' swill. For this son "was dead and is alive again; he was lost and is found" (Luke 15:32). The father is unflinchingly realistic about the deadly damage sin causes and rejoices in his son's spiritual rebirth.

Are You Lost?

We are all lost children who, like the prodigal son, have wasted what God has lavished upon us. Our heavenly Father is also waiting for us to return home to him in repentance. Jesus assures us that our heavenly Father welcomes us back, no matter how long we have been away or how far we have wandered. He will compassionately embrace us and rejoice in our return with all the angels in heaven. Jesus says, "I tell you, there is rejoicing in the presence of the angels of God over one sinner who repents" (Luke 15:10).

When to Repent

You may think that you only need to repent after you have ignored God for a very long time or after you have committed some enormous sin. Or you may be waiting for all your "small" sins to add up before you confess them. Instead, we need to confess our unworthiness daily and ask God to be merciful to us (which he never tires of being) and to free us from the destructiveness of sin. After all, if we are to be channels of God's grace to others, we can't be clogged up with the daily sediment of sin.

After looking at stained-glass windows, one child described saints as "people the light shines through." She's right. But that means we need to be wiped clean of grime. Sin pollutes in subtle, almost imperceptible ways. Only God's continual forgiveness can wash us so clean that his light can shine through.

Locating Prayers of Confession and Pardon

The psalms are rich in confession. The classic one is Psalm 51 on *page 394* in the Prayer Book. David had not only committed adultery with Bathsheba but had also arranged for her husband to be killed. Only after Nathan the prophet confronted him, did David confess. (You can read the whole sordid story in 2 Samuel, Chapters 11 and 12.) Psalm 32 also speaks of the misery of being unrepentant, "When I kept silent, my bones wasted away," and of the peace and real joy that comes after confession is met with forgiveness *(see page 366* in the BCP). Daniel, a righteous man, also prays a great and memorable prayer of confession on behalf of his people. Look at Daniel 9:4b–11, 18–19. Best of all, the psalms speak of pardon, as in Psalm 103:8–14.

(cont'd on page 75)

Locating Prayers of Confession and Pardon *(cont'd)*

Throughout the Prayer Book you can find prayers of confession and pardon. Always the one is followed by the other; for as the psalmist declared, "there is forgiveness with thee" (Psalm 130:4). We will look at the General Confession in the Daily Offices *(4, 19)* on page 153. **The Litany** *(30)* has a powerful penitential component. We will discuss the whole service on page 128. There is a different General Confession in **Holy Communion** *(77)*, and the "O Lamb of God" anthem *(84)* sung during Communion is deeply penitential.

The **Ministry to the Sick** *(576)* allows for both a general confession and, "if the sick person feels his conscience troubled with any weighty matters," for making a special confession heard privately by the priest *(581)*. There is a whole service of confession and pardon called simply **A Penitential Service** *(613)* that can be used on Ash Wednesday and at other times. There are also brief but straightforward confessions and prayers of pardon in the **Service for Young People** *(622)*, in **Compline** *(726)*, and in **Family Prayer** *(730)*.

Thanksgiving: Which Leper Are You?

As Jesus was going into a village, ten men who had leprosy met him. They stood at a distance and called out in a loud voice, "Jesus, Master, have pity on us!" When he saw them, he said, "Go, show yourselves to the priests." And as they went they were cleansed. One of them, when he saw that he had been healed, came back, praising God in a loud voice. He threw himself at Jesus' feet and thanked him—and he was a Samaritan. Jesus asked, "Were not all ten cleansed? Where are

the other nine? Was no one found to return and give praise to God except this foreigner?" Then he said to him, "Rise and go; your faith has made you well."

(LUKE 17:12–19)

Are We One of the Nine?

Like the nine lepers, we forget to thank God for all he has done. Ingratitude is a serious sin of omission. Greed grabs and never says "thank you." Gratitude takes nothing for granted. Too often we want the gifts but not a relationship with the Giver. George Herbert (1593–1633), an Anglican priest and poet, noted for his humility, energy, and charity, wrote, "You have given me so much. Give one thing more, a grateful heart."

In our culture, a sense of entitlement beats out gratitude. "I deserve this." "You owe me one." Yet even our talents are God-given. We are quick to dwell on past slights, but can't recall past kindnesses. Memory is a vital part of thanksgiving. We cannot say thanks with short memories. Yet grateful memories will carry us through the darkest of times.

Whiners and Grumblers

The people of God in the Old Testament were told constantly to remember what God had done for them. When the Israelites forgot God's graciousness, they became whiners and grumblers. First they forgot God's goodness towards them and then they forgot God himself. Perhaps we need to compose a personal psalm of thanksgiving, recalling all that God has done for us across our lives.

When we examine our conscience, it helps to think not just of specific sins such as pride, greed, or envy but of specific relationships. What sin tends to characterize each one? What is most needed to heal each relationship? Finally, what gift are we particularly thankful for in each relationship as we examine it in the light of gratitude? We should be as quick to thank God for the gifts we have received at his hand as we are to repent of various sins or to pray for certain needs.

Locating Prayers of Thanksgiving

Some of the great psalms of thanksgiving are 30, 34, 107, and 136. Jonah, too, prays a great song of thanksgiving while still in the belly of the great fish. Read the second chapter of Jonah. It is probably the only prayer in the Bible that ends with the Lord commanding a creature to vomit, which, from Jonah's point of view, is a good thing!

The BCP is full of thanksgivings. There is the amazing General Thanksgiving that covers a lot of ground in one

(cont'd on page 78)

Locating Prayers of Thanksgiving (cont'd)

prayer *(14)*. We will look more closely at it in Chapter Four, page 205. Many shorter prayers express gratitude for specific things: missions *(58)*; our national heritage and Confederation *(59)*; the Commonwealth *(60)*, deliverance from peril *(60, 636)*; favourable weather *(60)*; the ending of civil or industrial strife *(61)*; recovery from sickness *(61)* and the advancement of medical science *(61)*; thanksgiving after childbirth *(573–575)*; and the blessings of a harvest *(617–620)*. The Prayer Book draws to a close on its last page with a prayer that thanks God, "for power to work and leisure to rest, for all that is beautiful in creation and in the lives of men" *(736)*. There is also a wonderful thanksgiving after receiving Holy Communion in which "we thank thee that thou dost graciously feed us in these holy mysteries," in which we also offer to God "ourselves, our souls and bodies" which is, of course, a prayer of commitment *(85)*. The whole prayer is worth pondering.

Struggling With Supplication

Petition seems the easiest type of prayer to practice. We want something; we ask God for it. "Give us this day our daily bread" is the one part of the Lord's Prayer that we "get" or grasp quite naturally. Yet supplication poses several difficult problems. Are any of the following issues affecting your prayer life?

▶ If God already knows what we need and is going to do what he has already planned, why do we bother asking?

"Ye have not because ye ask not" (James 4:2, KJV). God invites us to ask of him, so we obey. Petitionary prayer is not only permitted, it is commanded. That is one of the mysteries of prayer.

▶ Are we leaving God out of our lives because we don't pray to him about what is really troubling us?

Do we pray about Aunt Hetty's upcoming knee operation, but resist praying about another, closer relationship that gives us deep, personal grief? As Christians, we need to remember and acknowledge (which we do by praying to him) that God is part of every aspect of our lives. Too often we think we have a situation all figured out, but we forget to factor God in. Or when we think we'll never figure out a problem, when we're discouraged by all the known and unknown factors, we need to remember that God is part of the equation, and trust the Master Mathematician. Even when life doesn't seem to add up or when our troubles only seem to multiply, we need to turn to God in prayer. He will make the significant difference. We can never know the future, but we can learn to trust our future in his hands.

▶ Do we not know what to ask for, because we haven't thought our needs through clearly?

WANTS   **NEEDS**
TEMPORAL   **SPIRITUAL**
FOR ME   **FOR OTHERS**

Just as we tend to come to confession with only a vague sense of our sins, so we often come to supplication with only a vague idea of our needs. We need to be more specific. (This is not the same as having a shopping list of solutions.) We need to think clearly about our needs and, if we're still confused, to pray for clarity. "What do you want me to do for you?" Jesus asked Bartimaeus, the blind man who came to him to be healed. Bartimaeus knew. "Rabbi, I want to see" (Mark 10:51). Do we know what we want?

▶ Are we asking God to help us find solutions, or are we demanding that he make our ideas work?

We don't have to know the answers to our problems or the problems of others. God will have more innovative ideas, and we need to be open to them.

▶ Do we think that we cannot possibly bother God for temporal things; that only spiritual requests are worthy of his holy attention?

Jesus taught us to pray, "Give us this day our daily bread." Bread is pretty down-to-earth.

▶ Are we so focussed on temporal requests that we forget to pray for spiritual needs? No wonder we are spiritually impoverished!

"Man does not live on bread alone but on every word that comes from the mouth of God," Jesus said (Matthew 4:4). "If any lacks wisdom, let him ask God who gives generously to all... and it will be given to him" (James 1:5). This principle applies to any fruit of the Spirit: "Love, joy, peace, patience, kindness, goodness, faithfulness, gentleness and self-control" (Galatians 5:22). God is pleased when we ask for any of these good gifts.

▶ Do we lack confidence in God? Do we either doubt that he has the power to meet our needs, or doubt that he loves us enough to want to help us?

> Cast your cares on the Lord and he will sustain you.
> (PSALM 55:22)

> Cast all your anxiety on him, for he cares for you.
> (1 PETER 5:7)

▶ Do we give up asking too soon? Sometimes God is not saying "No," only "Not yet."

Jesus encourages us to be persistent in prayer by telling the story of a poor widow who kept badgering an unjust judge day and night until he became so annoyed, he gave her the judgement she asked for just to get rid of her (Luke 18:1–8). God is a just judge, who truly cares for us. Persistence is part of the discipline of supplication. If persistence prevails even with the unfair judge, who cares not for the oppressed, how much more will it prevail with our heavenly Father, who cares for the afflicted! Jesus assures us, "And will not God bring about justice for his chosen ones, who cry out to him day and night? I tell you, he will see that they get justice, and quickly" (Luke 18:7–8).

▶ Do we ask only for our own needs and ignore the needs of others?

> Bear ye one another's burdens.
> (GALATIANS 6:2, KJV)

> Pray at all times in the Spirit, with all prayer and supplication ... making supplication for all the saints [believers].
> (EPHESIANS 6:18, RSV)

▶ Do we want to manipulate or control God by trying to call all the shots?

We forget who is master. We cannot be control freaks with God or force his hand. Supplication is request, not command. It is "Please would you?", not "Do this now, exactly as I say!" C.S. Lewis said,

> The essence of request, as distinct from compulsion, is that it may or may not be granted. And if an infinitely wise Being listens to the requests of finite and foolish creatures, of course he will sometimes grant and sometimes refuse them.[8]

▶ Do we wonder if God really loves us when he answers "No"?

This is perhaps the toughest issue. Sometimes, looking back, we can see that many of our petitions were foolish and we're actually relieved that God said "No." Some refusals turn out to be great blessings in disguise. But there are other refusals that we cannot fathom, and never will this side of heaven.

The Gethsemane "No"

Jesus, in the garden of Gethsemane, on the night he was arrested, was "overwhelmed with sorrow to the point of death" and "fell with his face to the ground" as he prayed. St. Luke tells us he was in such anguish that "his sweat was like blood falling to the ground." He knew the crucifixion lay ahead, yet he pleaded to be spared such a bitter "cup." Mark tells us that he cried out, "Abba, Father, everything is possible for you. Take this cup from me. Yet not what I will, but what you will." Matthew tells us that the second and third time Jesus cried, "My Father, if it is not possible for this cup to be taken away unless I drink it, may your will be done."

Jesus didn't just resignedly think, "No point in telling my Father what I most fear. God wants me crucified, so I'll just go ahead." No. Jesus exposes his anguish honestly to his Father. He lays out all his terror, and asks if another course is possible. He wrestles with God. He is persistent; he asks three times. Each time he echoes the very prayer he taught us, "Thy will be done." So he aligns his will with his Father's, which is one definition of prayer. But such an aligning is not automatic. He already knew what the Father wanted him to do, but he still struggled with it.

So if the holiest of all petitioners was refused, we must not be surprised if God sometimes says "no" or "not yet" to us. Nor should we think God plays favourites and loves more those who receive favourable answers to their prayers. After all, God did not grant this request from his beloved Son, who perfectly pleased him.

You can read about Jesus' prayer struggle in Matthew 26:36–46, Mark 14:32–42, and Luke 22:39–46.

Sleepy Intercessors

Jesus asked his disciples to "keep watch and pray" with him on that terrifying night. Instead, they all fell asleep. He woke them up, but they fell asleep again. They couldn't watch with the Son of God for even one hour. We will sometimes be called upon to watch with those going through overwhelming sorrow. How faithful will we be?

As Christians, we should be open to saying to people, "I will pray for you." And of course, we must try to follow through. We may not be able to counsel people, but we can always pray for them. And for those who really irritate or frustrate us, prayer for their well-being may be our only hope in the relationship.

In praying for others, we need to be sensitive to what God may be asking us to do, perhaps in very practical ways, for them. This is the time to listen inwardly. God will not lay every burden on your heart, but he will lay some particular ones.

At the same time, we must not lift people up to God in prayer and still continue to worry ourselves sick about them. We should leave our burdens with God, just as we should leave our sins and guilt with him.

Christians who regularly pray for others know how vital it is to keep their focus on the Provider and Healer and not be overwhelmed by the needs of those for whom they are interceding. The intercessor keeps watch over the people prayed for but also looks expectantly to God to see what he will do.

Lament: Tears in the Temple

We do not have to be all smiles in prayer. The people of God are not expected to wear happy-face logos. Old Testament heroes such as Hannah and Hezekiah cried out in sharp anguish to God. Hannah was a godly, married woman but when she found herself barren she sought the Lord with tears in the Temple.

> In bitterness of soul Hannah wept much and prayed to the Lord. Eli [the priest] thought she was drunk [and scolded her]. She replied, "Not so, my lord. I am a woman who is deeply troubled. I have not been drinking wine or beer. I was pouring out my soul to the Lord… I have been praying here out of my great anguish and grief."
>
> (1 SAMUEL 1:10, 15, 16)

Funeral homes always provide plenty of boxes of tissues. Perhaps churches should keep a few handy. Priests need to be as ready for tears of grief as tears of joy. Certainly God is. If you read the first two chapters of 1 Samuel in the Old Testament, you will discover how God marvellously answered Hannah's prayers. She returns to the temple to sing a remarkable song of praise that celebrates the way that God reverses human expectations.

Men Cry Too

Hezekiah, one of the most godly kings of Judah, had it all: wealth, power, and respect. Then in his prime, he "became ill and was at the point of death." Even the great prophet Isaiah told him, "This is what the Lord says, 'Put your house in order, because you are going to die. You will not recover.'"

Hezekiah turned his face to the wall and prayed to the Lord. "Remember, O Lord, how I have walked before you faithfully and with wholehearted devotion and have done what is good in your eyes." And Hezekiah wept bitterly.

Then God directed Isaiah, "Go back and tell Hezekiah … 'I have heard your prayer and seen your tears. I will heal you.'" You can read Hezekiah's story in 2 Kings, Chapter 20.

When You're Angry at God

God counts all our tears (Psalm 56:8). The language of prayer is not just joyful praise and thanksgiving. It is also bitter complaint and lament. Look at the opening verses of Psalm 142:

> I cry aloud to the Lord;
> I lift up my voice to the Lord for mercy.
> I pour out my complaint before him;
> before him I tell my trouble.

There are probably more psalms of lament and complaint in the Bible than of joy! Look particularly at Psalms 13, 22, 25, 42, 43, and 69. In the BCP, **A Supplication** *(35)* is a special prayer for "times of trouble." We will speak more of it in Chapter Three, p. 131. For now, note how, in its litany, we ask God,

> Graciously look upon our afflictions
> Pitifully behold the sorrows of our hearts. *(36)*

---

pitifully: with pity

A Cry for Help

Lament is a cry for help. Like the psalmist, talk with God about your disappointments and hurts, your anger and frustrations, and even your hates. He can take it all. Too often we bottle up these unpleasant emotions until they either explode or burst inward, and wreak havoc. Or we complain to everyone but God. He knows what's going on *but he wants to hear it from us.*

Better to lay out all the messiness of our lives before him and let him sort it out. Better to be shouting angrily at God, entrusting him with our hurts, than to pretend nothing is wrong or to give him the stony, silent treatment. Lament, complain—but do so to God. Then listen attentively. Be open to receive what he has to say to you.

One preacher, Chris King, told his congregation: "In lament, our agony calls out in harmony with the agony of God." The congregation felt angry because the father of three small girls had been killed in a traffic accident. King preached these words at his funeral:

> We can speak our minds to God. We can ask our
> questions and scream our pain and attack him with our
> anger, and God, like a loving parent with a deeply
> distressed child, holds us in his embrace as we beat
> our fists on his chest and weep on his shoulder. And he
> goes on holding us in his loving embrace until the
> questions and anger melt and we are comforted.[9]

Some people may find it strange to talk about the "agony of God." But there is good biblical support for this kind of expression. We are told in Judges 10:16, "And he [God] could bear Israel's misery no longer." Isaiah speaks of God sorrowing over his people Israel even when they were stubborn or rebellious, when "In all their distress he [God] too was distressed, and the angel of his presence saved them" (Isaiah 63:9).

Our God is "afflicted in the afflictions of [his] people" as we pray in the prayer "For those in Anxiety." He is not only almighty and powerful, he is also tender and compassionate:

> Almighty God, *who art afflicted in the afflictions of
> thy people*: Regard with thy *tender compassion* those
> in anxiety and distress; bear their sorrows and their
> cares; supply all their manifold needs; and help both
> them and us to put our whole trust and confidence in
> thee; through Jesus Christ our Lord. *Amen.*
>
> > *(54) [emphasis added]*

Friends in Need:
Adapting Biblical Prayers

St. Paul often breaks right into prayer in the middle of his letters to the churches. These prayers were for the Romans and the Philippians and the Ephesians. But we can pray them, too, for our family and friends. We may remember to pray for people when they are sick or in trouble, but Paul shows us that its good to pray at all times for other believers, remembering their spiritual needs.

Check out these prayers and insert the names of people you want to hold up to God in prayer. For instance, when you come to a "you," simply insert a friend's name like this:

> I bow my knees before the Father, from whom
> every family in heaven and on earth is named,
> that according to the riches of his glory he may
> grant *you, Lee* and *Marta*, to be strengthened
> with might through his Spirit in the inner man,
> and that Christ may dwell in your hearts through
> faith; that *you, Steve* and *Josie*, being rooted and
> grounded in love, may have power to comprehend
> with all the saints, what is the breadth and
> length and height and depth, and to know the
> love of Christ which surpasses knowledge, that
> *you, Carmen*, may be filled with all the fullness
> of God.
>
> [BASED ON EPHESIANS 3:14–19, RSV]

(cont'd on page 90)

Friends in Need: Adapting Biblical Prayers *(cont'd)*

Wow! Lee, Marta, Steve, Josie and Carmen couldn't ask for a much richer prayer! The whole prayer is Ephesians 3:14–21.

Try adapting these prayers to your friends' names:
1 Thessalonians 5:23
2 Thessalonians 2:16–17
Philippians 1:3–11
Colossians 1:9–12
Hebrews 13:20–21
Jude 24–25

You can decide whether to pray these prayers in the presence of your friends or offer them privately before God.

Locating More Prayers of Supplication

Jeremiah offers us a powerful prayer for healing and deliverance:

Heal me, O Lord, and I will be healed;
save me and I will be saved,
for you are the one I praise.

(JEREMIAH 17:14)

Many psalms cry out to God from a bed of pain and distress. Psalm 91 has been called the 911 emergency psalm! Here are some others: 23, 27, 31, 34, 42, 43, 71, 77, 86, 130, 142 and 146.

(cont'd on page 91)

Locating More Prayers of Supplication *(cont'd)*

There are numerous prayers of petition and intercession in the BCP. The longer ones gather many needs under one roof: A Prayer for all Conditions of men *(14)*; **The Litany**, especially the section beginning at the bottom of page *31*; A General Intercession *(57)*; A Bidding Prayer *(62)* which includes "Let us pray for... all who, through temptation, ignorance, helplessness, grief, trouble, dread, or the near approach of death, specially need our prayers"; and the Intercession in **Holy Communion** *(75)* which asks God to "comfort and succour all them, who in this transitory life are in trouble, sorrow, need, sickness, or any other adversity."

The shorter prayers of supplication focus on specific needs: for missions and outreach in **Prayers for Mid-day** *(16)*; for the Church and its mission *(13, 39–48)*; for the state *(12–13, 48–51)*; for agriculture, fisheries and industry *(51–54)*; and for people with various needs *(54–58)*, in this section, note especially "For those in Anxiety" *(54)*; for the people of God in the collects after Communion *(87–88)*, and in family morning prayer *(729)*; for married couples *(570–571)*; for those blessed with a new child *(575)*; after a miscarriage or stillbirth *(575)*; for those ill or dying *(55, 576–591)*; for those mourning *(55–57, 599–601)*; for those grieving the death of a child *(606–608)*; for young people and their teachers and parents *(47, 625–626, 732–734)*; for those in danger of storm *(635)*, battle *(51, 636)*, or hazardous occupations *(54)*; and for spiritual and physical protection *(11)*, especially for protection at night *(722–724, 726–727, 731)*.

The collects of the Christian Year *(94–330)* are also full of petitions, especially for our spiritual needs. See the Index on page 245 for a marvellous selection.

Are We Cheating God
When We Pray from a Prepared Text?

Hopefully, by now, you are convinced of the rightful place of adoration and confession, lament and petition, intercession and thanksgiving in a life of prayer. But you may not yet be convinced that a Christian is allowed to pray these elements from a prepared text, unless that text is Scripture itself.

Shouldn't our hearts just naturally overflow with praise and thanksgiving? Shouldn't we find our own words to express lament and confession? Can a prayer honestly be our own when we use someone else's words? How can their prayers really be ours? Aren't we being lazy and cheating God of Spirit-filled worship?

It is the Holy Spirit who brings life to a prayer, just as he brings life to a person. He infuses the words and he infuses us, for our bodies are his holy temple. When we don't know how to pray, he helps us (Romans 8:27).

We each have our own relationship with God, so we each will have our own personal conversation with him. Spontaneous prayer will be part of that dialogue. But we also have much in common in the family of God. Just as a great love song expresses the feelings of thousands who are in love, so a great prayer can find an echo in our own hearts. It is able to speak for us as if the words were our very own.

We should offer to God the best prayers that have been used by others. And as we pray them sincerely with the grace of the Holy Spirit, we make them our own.

Making the Prayers of Others Our Own

As a devout Jew, Christ prayed the psalms from memory. Psalm 22 was on his lips as he hung dying on the cross. He made David's prayer his own and pushed it beyond anything David ever imagined.

When we, too, are overwhelmed by fear or sorrow, or stirred by feelings of love or awe, we can pray using the words of other Christians. Their prayers can stimulate our own conversations with God. Fellow Christians can be our companions on the journey of prayer. Their worship can prompt an outpouring from our own souls. The great prayers of our faith can "jump-start" us into spontaneous prayer. Some of the truly great prayers of all ages are actually quite simple and direct, and get us talking to God.

Prayers That Percolate

In many translations of the psalms you will find included the word *Selah*. We're not sure what *Selah* means, but some scholars think it may be an instruction like "pause." Certainly, we need to pause from time to time in our prayers to reflect on what we've just said before we continue.

Instead of just rattling off the words, pause and ponder them. Listen to what God is personally saying to you. Let the prayer sink in, filtering down from your head to your heart. God often reaches our heads first, then touches our hearts. We need to let him affect our whole being.

Vain Repetition and Long-Winded Prayers

Jesus warns, "when you pray, do not be like the hypocrites, for they love to pray standing in the synagogues, and on the street corners, to be seen by men" (Matthew 6:5). They have all their reward. Instead, we should pray privately in our rooms.

Jesus is not saying we should never pray publicly in a house of prayer. After all, Jesus himself worshipped and taught in the synagogues. Nor does he mean we should never pray on the street corners. But wherever we pray, it should be humbly, to please God and not men. We are not to be spiritual show-offs:

> But when ye pray, use not vain repetitions, as the heathen do, for they think that they shall be heard for their much speaking.
>
> (MATTHEW 6:7, KJV)

Another translation reads:

> And in praying, do not heap up empty phrases as the Gentiles do, for they think they will be heard for their many words.
>
> (MATTHEW 6:7, RSV)

It is vain or empty phrases that are despised. Prayer is to be from the heart, not just the mouth. It is an intimate conversation with God, not an exhibition for other people. Long prayers do not impress God, but heartfelt prayers do. "For your Father knows what you need before you ask him" (Matthew 6:8). Jesus then teaches his disciples the Lord's Prayer. It has probably been repeated more than any other prayer in history—often carelessly, other times with intense devotion.

Long prayers are not wrong in themselves. Just before his arrest and torture, Jesus prays a chapter-length prayer in the Upper Room. You might want to read it because, in it, he prays for you. He pleads first for himself, then for his disciples, and finally for all believers in later generations—that's us! (See John 17.) So it is not the length of the prayer that counts but our spiritual attitude. Remember, God is not clocking us, he is listening to our hearts.

Short and to the Point

If you are expecting only long, rambling prayers and services in the BCP, you will be surprised. Some services are remarkably short, like the **Prayers at Mid-day** *(16)*, **Compline** *(722)*, and **Forms of Prayer to be Used in Families** *(728)*. Many prayers are only a brief paragraph long. Look at the concise collects on pages *124, 126, 134, 145, 147, 148, 196, 221, 224, 233, 242, 244, 247, 249, 252,* and *259.* Other prayers are simple petitions that, like the psalms they are drawn from, get straight to the point:

Priest: Give peace in our time, O Lord;
People: And evermore mightily defend us. *(11)*

The simple but powerful litany from the **Solemnization of Matrimony** is also used (with slight modifications) in the **Thanksgiving after Childbirth** and the **Ministry to the Sick:**

Minister: O Lord, save thy servant, and thy handmaid;
Answer: Who put their trust in thee.
Minister: O Lord, send them help from thy holy place;
Answer: And evermore defend them.
Minister: Be unto them a tower of strength;
Answer: From the face of their enemy.
Minister: O Lord, hear our prayer;
Answer: And let our cry come unto thee.

(569, modified on 574, 577)

So if you think short is sweet, there are prayers and services in the BCP for you. Start with the shorter prayers and psalms if you like, but eventually explore them all. Over half the psalms are short, twelve verses or less. Of course, some of the most magnificent psalms such as 19, 22, 27, 34, 42, 51, 91, 103, and 139 are longer than a dozen verses, but you will no doubt dip into them sooner or later. If you feel you can only get into the pool in the shallow end, then do so. We will have you swimming in the whole Psalter in no time.

Praying Across the Day with the Book of Common Prayer

Here we'll cover, among other things, **Forms of Prayer to be Used in Families**; Collects; **Mid-Day Prayer**; **Compline**; Spontaneous prayer; the Church year; **The Litany**; the psalm cycle; and organized Bible reading, in other words, everything but **Morning** and **Evening Prayer** (the Daily Offices). We will devote Chapter Four to those longer services.

"Permission" to Pray

You need to give yourself "permission" to pray. You need to allow yourself the luxury of time with God, even if it doesn't seem an efficient use of your time. Remember, any friendship takes time to grow. It cannot be rushed. And even a strong relationship withers when we don't continue to spend attentive time with the other person.

Prayer is not something the world values, except in dire emergencies. You, too, will be tempted to think daily prayer is a waste of time. You are not alone in this. The devil would rather have you off doing more "worthwhile" activities than getting to know God better.

But by breaking away to be with God each day, each Sunday, and occasionally for a retreat, you acknowledge his supremacy. This will allow you later to jump back into the rush of life with renewed vigour and perspective. You are not avoiding life when you pray, but you will be avoiding God, and missing opportunities to know him personally, when you don't pray.

A Still Space

Whether you say your devotions at home alone or with members of your family, choose a place where you'll have some privacy and will not be easily distracted. Find a place where you feel comfortable. You will soon find that God is waiting there for you. To protect your solitude, let your answering machine pick up your phone messages. You also need to find a stillness within yourself. Remember not to come out of prayer and contemplation too quickly. Take time to listen to God as you reflect on what you have prayed and read. It is much like cooling down in physical exercises.

We are told, "Be still and know that I am God" (Psalm 46:10).

We don't need the thunder of an organ or a multitude of voices to worship God. In St. John's vision, even in heaven, where there was "a great multitude that no one could count, from every nation, tribe, people, and language," worshipping God, when the seventh seal was opened, "there was silence in heaven for about half an hour" (Revelation 7:9, 8:1). It was a solemn silence.

A Quiet Whisper

When the prophet Elijah feared for his life, he fled to a cave. There God told him, "Go out and stand on the mountain in the presence of the Lord, for the Lord is about to pass by." Then a powerful wind tore mountains apart and shattered rocks, "but the Lord was not in the wind. After the wind there was an earthquake, but the Lord was not in the earthquake. After the earthquake came a fire, but the Lord was not in the fire" (1 Kings 19:11–12).

At Pentecost, the Holy Spirit descended in "a sound like the blowing of a violent wind from heaven" and "what seemed to be tongues of fire" separated and rested on each of the disciples (Acts 2:3). So God does manifest himself sometimes in wind and fire. But to the distraught Elijah, God revealed himself in something else: "And after the fire came a gentle whisper" or, as the King James Version describes it, "a still small voice" (1 Kings 19:12).

We, too, must not be afraid to rest quietly and trustfully with God:

> I have stilled and quieted my soul;
> like a weaned child with its mother
> like a weaned child is my soul within me.
>
> (PSALM 131:2)

Panic Attack

When hectic becomes frantic and we are thrust into overdrive, it is Jesus who says, "Peace, be still" (Mark 4:39, KJV). He sheds his powerful peace over our hearts and transforms our panic into peace. Prayer has been described as "the inward attentiveness to the Divine Whisper." God even sings a lullaby over us. Listen:

> The Lord your God is with you,
> he is mighty to save.
> He will take great delight in you,
> he will quiet you with his love,
> he will rejoice over you with singing.
>
> (ZEPHANIAH 3:17)

There is the cruel silence of two who are angry at each other, and who refuse to speak in each other's company. Then there is the comfortable silence of friends who have laughed and said much but who are now just relaxing in each other's presence. So yes, we listen for what God might say to us and reflect on what he has already said to us in Scripture, but we also simply delight in his presence.

Praying Aloud—Even in Private

If possible, you might consider praying aloud (not loudly but audibly). We tend to speed-read; a quick glance and we're done. Praying audibly will slow you down and prevent any surface dash over the text. As well, your ear will help you pick up and recover what might otherwise be lost. Your concentration will often increase when you hear yourself.

Sometimes in the psalms we address our souls: "Bless the Lord, O my soul" or "Why are you downcast, O my soul?" This plays better aloud. Of course, audible prayer can be just as mindless and heartless as silent prayer. We have to engage both mind and heart constantly.

Worship should include quiet pauses or moments of reflection, especially after a reading or an important prayer. A prayer needs to flow and not be disjointed, but a headlong dash to the final *Amen* doesn't edify anyone.

On the other hand, you needn't give equal weight to every word. Rather, in each prayer, try to savour at least one phrase. If each day you pause over a different phrase, you will gradually grasp the whole prayer. Pause at the end of your devotions, before you rush into your daily work, and let God talk with you.

We're ready now to take the plunge, and start looking at how to give structure and order to our daily prayer life. Let's jump right in, and see what the Book of Common Prayer has to offer.

Forms of Prayer for Families—or Anyone

One of the simplest ways to ease yourself into a daily rhythm of prayer is to take advantage of the **Forms of Prayer to be Used in Families,** found on *pages 728–736* in the BCP. These are brief morning and evening prayers that can be said in five to ten minutes, by individuals as well as by families. If you are just beginning the discipline of daily prayer, this is a great place to start.

A Wake-Up Call: Family Morning Devotions (728)

Many people mutter "O God!" when they first wake up, more as an unthinking moan than a prayer. They fear or despise what lies ahead. Look at the opening of the family morning devotions:

> O God, thou art my God, early will I seek thee. In the morning I will direct my prayer unto thee, and will look up.
>
> (PSALM 63:1, PSALM 5:3) *(728)*

Savour the first six words: "O God, thou art *my* God." We are praying a prayer of commitment, of love, of surrender to the One to whom we have entrusted our lives. We recommit ourselves to him daily. This phrase is worth praying when we awaken, during the first moments of consciousness while we still lie in bed. You won't need to open a book to remember those six or eleven words. And it won't be a curse we bring down on ourselves and our day, but a blessing. Even if you don't get to your full devotions until some time later, you will have started the day right.

This is the only daily service in the Book of Common Prayer that omits an explicit confession (except for "forgive us our trespasses" in the Lord's Prayer). The Prayer Book assumes that confession was made the night before. For a prayer of confession, turn over to the one on *page 730* and then add "For Pardon through the Cross" beneath it.

Then comes a "Thanksgiving for the gift of another day": "We give thee hearty thanks ... for the rest of the past night and the gift of a new day ..."

A Prayer for a Week

In both morning and evening devotions, praying the Collect of the day is suggested. The collect for each Sunday is usually prayed throughout the week. In this way, the prayer has time to sink into our souls. We can deepen our prayer life further by meditating on the daily collect. We'll talk more about collects under "Astonishing prayers that collect our thoughts" on page 105.

Next follows "Prayer and Intercession" with its wonderful light images. We pray, "Pour down upon us all the riches of thy grace" *(729)*. Notice the phrase, "Pour down," for this is a generous God of whom we can ask much, especially grace.

Then you can choose from a selection of additional prayers that are especially appropriate for families *(731–734)*. They include prayers not only for small children but also for adult offspring who may have left home *(733)*. There is even a birthday prayer *(734)*.

In a prayer "For Relatives and Friends," "for all who are near and dear to us," we ask that God would "awaken all who are careless about eternal things" and that we may "help, and not hinder, one another" in all good works *(732)*.

These morning devotions close with a superb prayer of dedication:

> O God, Most High and Holy, Three in One,
> Father, Son and Holy Spirit:
> We offer to thee this day
> Ourselves, our souls and bodies,
> To be a reasonable, holy and living sacrifice unto thee;
> To whom be all praise and glory. *Amen.*
>
> *(729)*

Look how closely this commendation follows St. Paul's own words to the Romans, "in view of God's mercy, ... offer your bodies as living sacrifices, holy and pleasing to God, this is your spiritual act of worship" (Romans 12:1).

Prayers to Sleep On: Family Evening Devotions (730)

The family evening devotions open with Psalm 141:2 *(730)*. The prayer "For Pardon through the Cross" is particularly worth noting, as is "For Freedom from Worry." The latter is ideal for the stressed-out Christian:

> O Lord, who hast pity for all our weakness: Put away
> from us worry and every anxious fear, that, having
> ended the labours of the day as in thy sight, and
> committing our tasks, ourselves, and all we love into thy
> keeping, we may, now that night cometh, receive as
> from thee thy priceless gift of sleep; through Jesus
> Christ our Lord. *Amen.*
>
> *(730)*

These family devotions close with several of the same verses as **Compline.** See page 110, where we will discuss the dark and

bright sides of "and at the last a perfect end."

Both your morning and your evening devotions can be filled out with additional prayers, taken from various places in the Book of Common Prayer. There are many prayers in the BCP that are easy to memorize, that we can recall whenever we need them over the course of the day—which leads us straight into a discussion of the collects.

Astonishing Prayers That Collect Our Thoughts

We can think of a collect (pronounced **COL**-lect) as a brief prayer that collects our thoughts. It is usually one long, flowing sentence that pours into a paragraph. Although it often has only one period, we need to pray it with pauses after the commas, if we want it to sink in. Anthony Burton, Bishop of Saskatchewan, has described collects as treasures that "flash, astonish, challenge, and delight."[10]

A typical collect consists of five parts:

1. the address to God
2. which is expanded by a description of the special grounds on which we approach him
3. the petition
4. the purpose of our petition
5. the closing, with a pleading of Christ's name or an acknowledgement of God's glory.

Here is one example:

1. O God,
2. who hast prepared for them that love thee such good things as pass man's understanding:
3. pour into our hearts such love towards thee
4. that we, loving thee above all things, may obtain thy promises, which exceed all that we can desire;
5. through Jesus Christ our Lord. *Amen.*

Sixth Sunday after Trinity (226)

Besides collects for different themes and purposes, there is a collect for each day of the Christian year *(94–330)*. These 122 collects are mostly distributed one for each Sunday and the following week, as well as for the various holy days and for special occasions in parish life.

To find collects for any theme or occasion, see the full index on page 245. Let's look at just two more here:

Invocation [call]   O God,

This is the problem: forasmuch as without thee we are not able to please thee:

So we ask [petition]:   Mercifully grant, that thy Holy Spirit may in all things direct and rule our hearts;

We plead in Christ's Name.   Through Jesus Christ our Lord, *Amen. Nineteenth Sunday after Trinity (249)*

Notice what this collect teaches us about Christian prayer:

1. Almighty and everlasting God,
2. who art always more ready to hear than we to pray, and art wont to give more than we either desire or deserve:
3. Pour down upon us the abundance of thy mercy;
4. forgiving us those things whereof our conscience is afraid, and giving us those good things which we are not worthy to ask,
5. but through the merits and mediation of Jesus Christ, thy Son, our Lord. Amen.

Twelfth Sunday after Trinity (236)

forasmuch as:	since
wont:	accustomed
whereof:	of which

Prayers for All Occasions (37–61)

Is your church dishonest at times, flawed, needy, or quarrelsome? Then pray this prayer "For the Church Universal":

Most gracious God, we humbly beseech thee for thy
holy Catholic Church. Fill it with all truth; in all truth
with all peace. Where it is corrupt, purify it; where it is in
error, direct it; where any thing is amiss, reform it; where
it is right, strengthen and confirm it; where it is in want,
furnish it; where it is divided and rent asunder, make it
whole again; through Jesus Christ our Lord. *Amen.*

(39)

This is the first of a rich treasury of almost sixty Prayers and
Thanksgivings that we can draw upon for both corporate
(congregational) and private worship *(37–61),* in addition to the
collects that we have already discussed. Other particularly notable
prayers are for peace in the world *(50–51),* for those in anxiety
(54), at the close of the day or "eventide" *(58),* and the General
Intercession *(57)* which we'll discuss later on page 202. There are
modern prayers here for industry *(53)* and the advancement of
medical science *(61).* Finally, there are collects in the **Communion**
service which are also superb prayers for any day *(87–88).*

Mission at Mid-day (16)

Mid-day is the briefest of all Prayer Book services *(16)*. The Lord's Prayer is followed simply by three short collects. It covers less than a page and a half and takes only two minutes to say. It would be a simple discipline at one's office desk at lunch. It focuses on three noontide events: Christ's crucifixion, St. Paul's conversion, and St. Peter's vision of God's compassion to the Gentiles. The theme is mission and reaching out beyond ourselves: "that all mankind may look unto thee [Christ] and be saved," "that all nations may come and worship thee," and "that we may fervently desire the salvation of all."

Mission is an excellent emphasis for noon, when we are most likely to be out working in the world. Of course, other prayers, both set and spontaneous, can be added. But using it to pierce our workday can be a superb grounding for what our life should be all about.

Holy Fear

The English poet and Anglican priest John Donne said, "Fear God and then none else." As Christians who trust in Jesus' redemptive death, we need fear neither man nor the coming judgement. But there is still a holy and reverential fear that is God-given. God takes our actions seriously. If we love him, we will fear to offend or grieve him. Holy fear enables us truly to honour God, obey his commands, and shun evil. So while we believe "God is love" (1 John 4:16), yet a reverent fear remains. Our God is awesome. Let's look next at **Compline,** which is a whole service of entrusting ourselves to this awesome God.

Compline: Trusting God through Night and Death *(722)*

Compline *(722)* is said just before retiring for the night. It was the last of the eight medieval daily services and so finished them. (For all eight services, see Chapter Four, page 142.) The name of the service comes from the Latin verb *complere*, "to fill up." Even in the twenty-first century, it will complete your day. This jewel of a service can be said in about ten minutes, so it is an easy but rewarding discipline. It is a favourite practice at conferences and retreats. If you have difficulty sleeping, try **Compline** instead of sedatives.

In worship we entrust ourselves and those we love to God. In morning devotions we commit the day ahead to God and in evening prayers we commit the night ahead to him. Sometimes, it is hard to let go of the past day, to entrust all its loose ends to our heavenly Father to sort out, and just rest in his arms, but that is what the evening services encourage us to do.

Compline opens with a line that seems soothing at first, as we slip into bed, but is actually quite dramatic when you unpack it:

> The Lord grant us a quiet night and a perfect end.

"Quiet night"—yes, we want that—"and a perfect end"? But what's this perfect end? In the **Family Evening Prayers,** the line is expanded to "and at the last, a perfect end." An older version doesn't mince words: "The Lord grant us a quiet night and a perfect death." "Whoa!" you say, "I thought I was slipping into sleep, not death!" Before you grab the tranquillizers, let's look at how this can be comforting.

A Good Death

The Book of Common Prayer, like the Bible upon which it is based, is unflinchingly realistic. Unless the Lord returns first, one of these days—or nights—we will most certainly die. From a Christian perspective, the horror is not in death itself, but in a death for which we are not spiritually prepared.

A perfect end for a Christian is a death we are ready for, because we have made our peace with God and with our fellow mortals. In **The Litany** we pray that God would spare us from sudden death, that is, a death that has not allowed us time to forgive those who have wronged us and seek God's forgiveness for our sins *(31)*. A good death is one in which we have got our spiritual house in order. **Compline** reminds us, right up front, to keep our spiritual house in order.

Rest for Our Souls

Compline offers us three scriptural sentences. Let's look at the middle one. Jesus invites "all ye that labour and are heavy laden" to come to him, for "ye shall find rest for your souls." After a hard day's work, this passage is particularly attractive, but notice how Jesus promises this rest. It is as we are hitched up to him in his work that we will find rest!

"Take my yoke upon you ..." A yoke is a wooden cross-piece which is fastened over the necks of two oxen and then attached to the plough or wagon which they are to pull. Christ invites us to join him in his work. Yet he assures us, "My yoke is easy and my burden is light." And so it is when we realize who shares it with us.

Into Thy Hands, O Lord

In his very last words on the cross, Christ cries out in a loud voice, "Father, into thy hands I commend my spirit" (Luke 23:46, KJV). We, too, now say three times, "Into thy hands, O Lord, I commend my spirit" and a fourth time, "I commend my spirit" (Psalm 35:5). We entrust our spirits to God's keeping. This is unmistakably a prayer of surrender.

Nightmare Alley

Note the constant plea throughout this bedtime service, "guard us," "keep us," "hide us," "preserve us," and "defend us." We also implore our Creator and Father to "be our guard and keeper now" in the ancient Latin hymn "Before the ending of the day." Some of us have difficulty falling asleep, difficulty giving our work, our cares, and our loved ones over to God. Others fear a sleep that warps into "ill dreams" and nightly fears and terrors. So we ask God to "tread under foot our ghostly foe," the devil *(723)*.

Then we ask God to cherish us, "Keep us as the apple of an eye" and protect us, "Hide us under the shadow of thy wings" (Psalm 17:8). The *Nunc Dimittis*, which we will explore later on page 214, is framed by a repeated anthem or poetic song:

> Preserve us, O Lord, waking, and guard us sleeping,
> that awake we may watch with Christ, and asleep we
> may rest in peace.

As in a lullaby, there is much gentle repetition in **Compline.**

We Bless God and He Blesses Us

Later, we praise God responsively, proclaiming, "Blessed art thou ..." To bless God is to praise him. "Bless" is the English word that was used to translate the Latin *benedicere*, "to say good of someone." When we bless God, we praise him as holy. When we ask him to bless us, we are not asking him to praise us but to grant us his favour and make us holy. When God blesses someone or something, he consecrates and sets apart that person or object, for his own use. And when we say we are blessed, as Mary does in the *Magnificat (21)*, we mean we are set apart for God and favoured by him. We, like Mary, Jesus' mother, are happy to receive his favour or blessing.

Celestial Brightness: The Collects of Compline

Compline is prayed at an hour when it may be hard to concentrate. Thankfully, there is not one lengthy prayer in the whole service. Its canticle, *Nunc Dimittis*, has only three lines and one of the psalms recommended, Psalm 134, has only four verses. There are six sets of prayer responses that are sharp and to the point, shot like arrows heavenward. But best loved are the glorious collects. Only one of the five need be said, but they are all superb.

The first, the Collect for Protection, invites the Lord to visit our place of rest and drive from it "all the snares of the enemy; let thy holy angels dwell herein to preserve us in peace" *(726)*.

Or we could choose the second and shortest one, "Lighten our darkness, we beseech thee, O Lord …" which is also the Collect for Aid against all Perils in **Evening Prayer** *(24)*.

The next three are optional *(727)*. The first may seem too macabre for modern sensibilities, speaking as it does of sepulchres, graves, and lying in the dust. This prayer came back into common use in World War I, to help soldiers at the front deal with the carnage. If you want something brighter, then try this lightning flash:

> Look down, O Lord, from thy heavenly throne;
> illuminate the darkness of this night with thy celestial
> brightness, and from the sons of light banish the deeds
> of darkness, through Jesus Christ our Lord. *Amen.*

The final collect of **Compline** seems to almost repose upon God's breast. It recognizes our human exhaustion, and acknowledges that in the midst of all the risks and changes of this transitory life, God alone offers security and rest:

Be present, O merciful God, and protect us through the silent hours of this night, so that we who are wearied by the changes and chances of this fleeting world, may repose upon thy eternal changelessness, through Jesus Christ our Lord. *Amen.*

There are two other fine evening collects in the Prayer Book, "At Eventide" *(58)*, and "For Freedom from Worry" *(730)*, both of which we have discussed already.

Compline, like most Prayer Book services, opens and closes with Scripture. Psalm 4:8 is the final refrain, pluralized to recognize the community of believers entrusting themselves to God: "We will lay us down in peace and take our rest; /For it is thou, Lord, only, that makest us dwell in safety."

Prayer on the Run

We can pray the collect "For Remembrance of God's Presence" *(731)* at the start of the day or at midday. But once the Prayer Book is closed and we are busy in our homes and in the world, how should we pray? We can simply lift people up to God by face or name and ask him to bless them. This brief style of intercession can be practised across the day.

Pray:
- ▶ for a person or issue that you read of in the newspaper
- ▶ for family members as you enter or pass their rooms
- ▶ for the recipient of a letter as you mail it
- ▶ for neighbours as you pass their homes
- ▶ for a sales clerk or store owner as you shop
- ▶ for health-care workers and patients as you pass a hospital
- ▶ for teachers and students as you pass a school
- ▶ for a congregation as you pass a church
- ▶ for someone wearing a cross
- ▶ for artists or musicians as you enjoy their work
- ▶ for the unknown person calling as the phone rings
- ▶ for the stricken when you hear an ambulance siren
- ▶ for mourners as you pass a cemetery
- ▶ for fellow workers as you pass their offices
- ▶ for someone you will e-mail as the computer boots up

When a stranger who passes you on the street reminds you of someone you know, pray for both the stranger and your friend. After talking with people, even people you dislike, hold them up to God in prayer, at least briefly. They need never know you are praying for them, but your attitude to them will soften with prayer.

We may hate line-ups, but they, too, can be places of prayer. Of course, arrow prayers, prayers shot quickly heavenward, are best when we're in the fast lane. Behind the wheel of a car or operating heavy equipment, we have to stay focussed. Long, complex prayers would be dangerous, but simple arrow prayers of only a few words would not distract.

Try these brief arrow prayers:

Go ahead of us, O Risen Lord.

Create in me a clean heart, O God. (PSALM 51:10, KJV)

Lord, I believe. Help thou
    mine unbelief. (MARK 9:24, KJV)

Lord, save me. (MATTHEW 14:30)

Lord, he whom you love is ill. (JOHN 11:3, RSV)

Abba, Father. (MARK 14:36)

God, be merciful to me a sinner. (LUKE 18:13, KJV)

Lord, you know that I love you. (JOHN 21:16)

Wherever I go—only Thou! Jewish prayer

O Lord, make me after your own heart. Brother Lawrence

Arrow Prayers from the BCP

Here are some prayers from the BCP that would be easy to memorize, and say very quickly:

Heaven and earth are full of thy glory.   *(79)*

Our help is in the name of the Lord;
Who hath made heaven and earth.   *(538)*

Blessed be the name of the Lord;
Henceforth, world without end.   *(538)*

Defend, O Lord, this thy servant
with thy heavenly grace.   *(560)*

Be unto them a tower of strength.   *(570)*

Peace be to this house, and to
all that dwell in it.   *(576)*

O Saviour of the world, who by thy Cross
and precious Blood hast redeemed us
Save us and help us.   *(578)*

The Lord be in thy heart and on thy lips.   *(581)*

Graciously look upon our afflictions, O Lord.
Pitifully behold the sorrows of our hearts.   *(598)*

Rest eternal grant unto him, O Lord,
and let light perpetual shine upon him.   *(601)*

The eyes of all wait upon thee, O Lord.   *(735)*

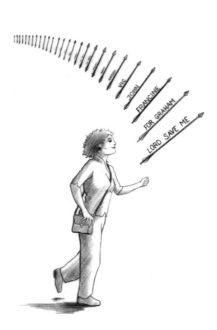

The Practice of the Presence of God

Even in the busyness of the day, we can offer up ourselves and others to the Lord. We can also lift up our work to him. Whether we are washing pots and pans or programming satellites, we can do it all for the Lord. "Whatever you do, do it all for the glory of God" (1 Corinthians 10:31).

Brother Lawrence (*c.* 1605–1691), a lay Carmelite brother, was put in charge of the kitchen in a monastery in Paris in 1649. He was noted for his prayerful life amid the constant clamour. He thought of himself as continually in the presence of God. He wrote:

> Think often on God, by day, by night, in your business, and even in your diversions. He is always near you and with you; leave Him not alone. You would think it rude to leave a friend alone who came to visit you; why then

must God be neglected? Do not, then, forget Him but
think on Him often, adore Him continually …[11]

Brother Lawrence was not recommending complex theological
thought but "little internal adorations." He taught:

A little lifting of the heart suffices, a little remembrance
of God, one act of inward worship, though upon a
march, and a sword in hand, are prayers, which,
however short, are nevertheless very acceptable to God.

The time of business does not differ from the time of
prayer; and in the noise and clatter of my kitchen, while
several persons are calling for different things, I possess
God in as great tranquillity as if I were upon my knees
at the Blessed Sacrament.[12]

Another Christian took a different approach to the busyness of
his day. In 1642, before the Battle of Edgehill, the first pitched
battle of the English Civil War, Sir Jacob Astley prayed, "O Lord,
thou knowest how busy I must be this day; if I forget thee, do
not thou forget me: for Christ's sake."[13]

Christ's Time for the Church

So far, we have talked mostly about the daily rhythm of prayer.
But just as there is a daily rhythm, so there should also be a
yearly rhythm of prayer. When we celebrate family birthdays and
anniversaries, our family imprints its life on us and reminds us of
our family identity. When we mark national holidays, our country
imprints its life on us and reminds us that we are its citizens. The
Christian year reminds us that Christ's life is imprinted upon
ours. We are part of God's family and are also citizens of the
Kingdom of Heaven.

As Christians our lives are shaped by Christ's life. "I have been crucified with Christ and I no longer live, but Christ lives in me," said St. Paul (Galatians 2:20). The church year marks Christ's birth, his temptation in the wilderness, his suffering, death and resurrection, and his ascension into heaven. It also celebrates the descent of the Holy Spirit at Pentecost (when the Church was born) and the Trinity.

The box below provides a quick overview of the Christian year *(93)*, as it has been celebrated for two millennia. It begins not on January 1 but with the first Sunday in Advent, the fourth Sunday before Christmas Day (which falls between November 27 and December 3).

The Christian Year *(93)*

Day or Period	Event(s) commemorated
Advent *(four weeks)*	Preparation for Christ's first and second coming
Christmas Day Sundays after Christmas *(one or two)*	Christ's birth
Epiphany, January 6 *(season lasts six weeks)*	Manifestation of Christ to the Gentiles
Ash Wednesday *(first day of Lent)*	

(cont'd on page 122)

The Christian Year *(cont'd)*

Lent *(forty weekdays before Easter)* Palm Sunday *(Sixth Sunday in Lent)* Begins the two-week Passiontide	Christ's 40 days in the wilderness
Holy Week including Good Friday	Christ's suffering (Passion) and death
Easter Day Five Sundays after Easter	Christ's resurrection
Ascension Day *(fortieth day after Easter)* One Sunday after Ascension	Christ's ascent into heaven
Pentecost *(fiftieth day after Easter)*	Descent of the Holy Spirit
Trinity Sunday *(Sunday after Pentecost)* Sundays after Trinity *(about 25 weeks)*	Celebration of the Trinity

The first half of the Christian year sets forth the great events and doctrines or teachings of the faith. The second half, after Trinity, teaches us practical responses to what God has accomplished for us in Christ. The post-Trinity collects are brief requests for spiritual grace.

The BCP sets aside other Holy Days *(260–330)* to commemorate great saints or important events such as the Annunciation—the angel's announcement to Mary that she would conceive the Christ Child by the power of the Holy Spirit, March 25 *(271)* —and the Transfiguration of our Lord, when Jesus was revealed in his heavenly glory while still on earth, August 6 *(289)*.

A Prayer for a Season

Earlier in this chapter, we saw that there is a special collect appointed for every week in the year. In addition to these, there are a few collects that are prayed for a whole season in the Christian year. These seasonal collects lend rich colour to our prayer life and are part of the genius of Anglican devotion. For instance, the powerful Collect for the First Sunday in Advent *(95)*, which speaks of Christ's first and second comings, is prayed during the four weeks of Advent until Christmas Eve:

Almighty God, give us grace that we may cast away the
works of darkness, and put upon us the armour of light,
now in the time of this mortal life, in which thy Son Jesus
Christ came to visit us in great humility; that in the last
day, when he shall come again in his glorious Majesty, to
judge both the quick [living] and the dead, we may rise
to the life immortal; through him who liveth and reigneth
with thee and the Holy Spirit, now and ever. *Amen.*

(95)

The majestic collect for the first day of Lent, Ash Wednesday
(138), is prayed for all the forty days of Lent until Holy Week.
The Collect for Christmas Day *(104)* is prayed for the twelve days
of Christmas, until the Eve of Epiphany. These prayers give a
distinct flavour to the seasons of Advent, Lent, and Christmas.

So each Sunday will have at least one particular collect that is
usually prayed throughout the week. During special times such as
the week before Easter (Holy Week), special collects take
precedence. The collect for Rogation Sunday (the Sunday before
Ascension) is said only until the Wednesday. Then beginning on
Thursday, which is Ascension Day, the collect for Ascension Day
is said for the rest of the week. So all days in the Christian year
have at least one collect and some have two. (Instructions for
when these special collects are to be said are found in small print
underneath them in the Prayer Book.)

The Collect for Ash Wednesday (138)

In just one sentence this collect can teach us much about true
repentance and God's amazing mercy! It is well worth praying
throughout Lent or whenever we need to grasp a better
understanding of forgiveness:

Almighty and everlasting God, who hatest nothing that
thou hast made, and dost forgive the sins of all them
that are penitent [repentant]: Create and make in us
new and contrite [truly sorry] hearts, that we, worthily
lamenting our sins, and acknowledging our
wretchedness, may obtain of thee, the God of all
mercy, perfect remission and forgiveness; through
Jesus Christ our Lord. *Amen.*

(138)

Hanging Out with Holy Mentors

Many holy days, like All Saints' Day *(299)* on November 1, recall
the saints who surround us and who encourage us by their
example and strengthen us by their fellowship. Several saints have
their own days. St. Mary Magdalene *(286)* is remembered on
July 22. The collects for St. Stephen the Martyr, December 26
(108), and the Innocents, December 28 *(111)*, can be used to
intercede for the persecuted church around the world:

Grant, O Lord, that in all our sufferings here upon
earth, for the testimony of thy truth, we may steadfastly
look up to heaven, and by faith behold the glory that
shall be revealed; and, being filled with the Holy Spirit,
may learn to love and bless our persecutors, by the
example of thy first Martyr Saint Stephen, who prayed
for his murderers to thee, O blessed Jesus, who
standest at the right hand of God to succour [help] all
those that suffer for thee, our only Mediator and
Advocate. *Amen.*

For Saint Stephen the Martyr (108)

We proclaim in the Apostles' Creed that we believe in the
Communion of Saints. These collects and lessons help us "hang

out," as it were, with saintly role models and mentors. They are not like worldly sports celebrities who are full of themselves and who keep their distance to keep their aura. They are the "faithful departed" who draw near to us to cheer us on in our own race, that we, like them, might finish well.

In the collect for All Saints' Day *(299)*, we acknowledge that God has "knit" us together with the saints in the mystical body of Jesus Christ. We ask that we might follow their good examples and eventually "come to those unspeakable [indescribable] joys which thou hast prepared for them that unfeignedly [truly] love thee." There are also three general collects on *page 56* thanking God for "all thy servants who have finished their course in thy faith and fear" and asking that we might with them be "partakers of the inheritance of the saints in light" and "at the last enter with them into the fullness of thine unending joy."

New Year, Fresh Start

The BCP doesn't ignore the civic year. Canada Day *(278, 281)* and Remembrance Day *(301)* both have special collects and lessons. There is also a wonderful prayer for the New Year *(115)* that is so good it is worth adapting for each new season or month, or whenever you need a fresh start:

> O Immortal Lord God, who inhabitest eternity, and hast brought thy servants to the beginning of another year [season, month]: Pardon, we humbly beseech thee, our transgressions in the past, bless to us this New Year [season, month], and graciously abide with us all the days of our life; through Jesus Christ our Lord. *Amen.*
>
> *(115)*

Fasting and Feasting

In this yearly cycle of prayer come times of both fasting and feasting. Our secular culture seems to overeat and then go on fad diets, pursuing first gluttony and then vanity. Christians, too, feast and fast but in the hope of being more God-centred. Ash Wednesday and Good Friday are the major *fast* days in the Anglican Church. All the Fridays of the year, except Christmas Day and Epiphany when they fall on Fridays, are days of *abstinence*, as are the forty days of Lent. In contrast, Christmas Day, Easter, and Pentecost are major *feast* days. We can worship God by how we eat.

Jesus taught his disciples saying "*When* you fast," not "*If* you fast." Fasting is not an optional discipline. See Matthew 6:16. And remember, Jesus also feasted!

When we *fast*, we restrict ourselves to at most one full meal, usually in the evening, and consume nothing or only light food such as a piece of toast or a bowl of soup for the rest of the day. We reduce our consumption but never to the point of causing bodily harm. Young children, the sick, the old, and pregnant and nursing women should not fast. *Abstinence* means giving up certain foods (such as meat) or drinks (such as wine) or treats (such as candy) completely on Fridays and for the forty days of Lent. In both fasting and abstinence, we avoid thoughtless indulgence and discern the goodness of God.

Fasts and feasts are all aspects of embodied prayer. Feast days are all the more appreciated after fasts, but whether we are eating rich or simple fare, we should give thanks to God. Several forms for prayer at mealtimes are provided in the Book of Common Prayer *(735)*.

And Now for Something Completely Different! The Litany *(30)*

If you need a complete change of pace, the majesty of **The Litany** *(30)* will sweep you away. This beautiful intercessory prayer has a thoroughness few others can match. It consists of a series of petitions that in church are recited by the leader and affirmed by the congregation in recurring phrases such as "Good Lord, deliver us" or "We beseech thee, good Lord." Beseech means "to beg earnestly or entreat."

There are six sections to **The Litany.** In the first, we call upon each person of the Trinity to have mercy upon us. We then conclude, "O holy, blessed and glorious Trinity, three persons and one God: have mercy upon us." Adoration and confession, awe and humility, are juxtaposed in echoing refrains.

Next we ask God to "remember not" our offences nor the sins of our ancestors, but by "thy most precious blood" to "Spare us, Good Lord."

The Four Last Things

Nor does **The Litany** shy away from the Four Last Things: Death and Judgement, Heaven and Hell. Most postmodernists only take death, the first of the four, seriously. For them, death is all there is. But Christians believe there will also be a day of judgement, after which some will go to everlasting condemnation and others, by faith in Christ's redeeming blood, to everlasting joy. So we pray that God will deliver us "from the crafts and assaults of the devil, from God's wrath and from everlasting condemnation." Later we will pray for God to deliver us "in the hour of death, and in the day of judgement."

In the third section, we name the evils and dangers from which we earnestly desire God to deliver us. The list of sins could also be used when we are examining our conscience: blindness of heart, pride, vainglory, hypocrisy, envy, hatred, malice, uncharitableness, uncleanness in thought, word and deed, the deceits of the world, the flesh and the devil, false doctrine, heresy, schism, hardness of heart, and contempt for God's Word. From all these we pray again and again, "Good Lord, deliver us."

vainglory:	extreme vanity, boastfulness
heresy:	a false teaching or belief
schism:	divisions within the church

We are not only vulnerable beings spiritually, but also physically; so we entreat God to deliver us, "from lightning and tempest, from earthquake, fire and flood, from plague, pestilence, and famine, from battle and murder and from sudden death," for which we are not spiritually prepared.

It is trusting in Christ's obedient life and death that saves a Christian. The **Litany** lays it out for us: "By the mystery of thy holy Incarnation, by thy holy Nativity, by thy Baptism, Fasting and Temptation, by thine Agony and bloody Sweat, by thy Cross and Passion [suffering], by thy precious Death and Burial, by thy glorious Resurrection and Ascension, by the sending of thy Holy Spirit, by thy heavenly Intercession [Jesus in heaven prays for us!], and by thy Coming again in glory, Good Lord, deliver us."

The next petition speaks of our life: "In all times of tribulation; in all times of prosperity; in the hour of death, and in the day of judgement, Good Lord, deliver us." It might strike you as odd that we ask God to deliver us "in all times of prosperity." Yet it is often during the good times that we forget God and lose our spiritual bearings. So we pray not to lose our intimacy with God in the midst of success (read Deuteronomy 6:10–12).

Mighty and Meek

In the fifth and longest section, we intercede for both the powerful and the weak. We pray for those who rule over us and serve us in church and state. And we pray for the vulnerable: travellers, women in labour, the sick and young children, prisoners, widows and orphans, and those who are desolate and oppressed. We pray for those who are spiritually lost, weak, or deceived, and ask that God would "beat down Satan under our feet."

Forgiveness is a distinguishing mark of Christianity; so we ask God, "To forgive our enemies, persecutors, and slanderers and to turn their hearts." We ask God to forgive us and also forgive those who have sinned against us. Does this comprehensive litany leave anything out?

It closes with a beautiful series of petitions asking Christ our Lord, the Son of God, the Lamb of God, to hear us and have mercy upon us. This is repeated not because we doubt God's mercy but because, as forgiven creatures, we need always to be in a state of humility and grace before our Maker.

In Times of Devastation: A Supplication (35)

How should we pray when our city or nation is plunged into a time of terror or grief, when evil seems to stalk the land? Perhaps a natural disaster has struck, a fire, flood, or earthquake, a famine or disease. Perhaps the tragedy is man-made, involving war, terrorism, or bloodshed. Whatever the devastation, God tells us to call upon him in the day of trouble, and so we do.

No one wants trouble, but when it comes, we want God to walk with us through it. God promises he will, "When he calls to me,

I will answer him; I will be with him in trouble, I will rescue him and honour him" (Psalm 91:15, RSV).

So in **A Supplication** *(35)* we call upon God to "arise" like a mighty warrior (Psalm 68:1). Three times we plead, "O Lord, arise, help us, and deliver us for thy Name's sake/for thine honour," not because we deserve his protection by virtue of our own goodness but because God has mercifully accepted us as his people. We cast ourselves upon his care.

We recall God's deliverance in times past and ask him to act powerfully now in our own day. We unburden all our "afflictions, sorrows, sins, infirmities, troubles, adversities, persecutions and the evils worked against us." Christ bore both our sins and our sorrows upon the cross. Our God is both a sin-bearer and a sorrow-bearer, a God of mercy and of consolation. By ourselves or with the whole congregation we cry out to God in a series of petitions. Here are four of them:

> From our enemies defend us, O Christ;
> Graciously look upon our afflictions.
> Pitifully behold the sorrows of our hearts;
> Mercifully forgive the sins of thy people. *(36)*

Next follow two collects. In the first, we ask God to turn all evil away from us, even the evil we have brought upon ourselves. We also ask that we may completely trust him in the midst of all our troubles. In the second collect, we ask "that those evils which the craft and subtlety of the devil or man worketh against us, be brought to naught [come to nothing]," and "be dispersed," and that we may be hurt by no persecutions.

The **Supplication** is worded in general terms. Specific prayers can be added such as "In Time of Dearth" [scarcity] and "Famine" *(53);* "Prayer in Respect of a Storm" *(635);* "Prayer with Respect to the Enemy" *(636);* or "For Peace in the World" *(50–51),* in which we ask, "that the day may be hastened when war shall be no more."

Later, after God brings us through the ordeal, we need to give thanks. We could pray, "For Deliverance in Peril" *(60),* in which we confess that "it is thy goodness alone that hath preserved us," "For the Ending of Civil or Industrial Strife" *(61)* or "Thanksgiving for deliverance" *(636)* from the recent peril.

We can meet God even in the abyss of despair. He walks with us through crisis and calm.

The Psalm Cycle

Every Christian should consider praying one or more psalms daily. To help you acquire this habit, the Book of Common Prayer moves you through these Old Testament prayers on a monthly cycle. Turn to *page 331,* and you will find the psalms divided into "The First Day: Morning Prayer," then on *page 335,* "The First Day: Evening Prayer," etc. These are the psalms appointed to be said at services of **Morning** and **Evening Prayer** on each day of the month.

Some find a bimonthly cycle more manageable. (See the chart on *page lv.*) The actual number of psalms varies each day because the psalms vary in length. (The longest, Psalm 119, is read over three days in the monthly cycle and six days in the bimonthly cycle.) Others cover the psalms every two months by praying the morning psalms in January, March, May, etc., and the evening psalms in February, April, June, etc.

The one-month or even the two-month cycle can be heavy going for new Christians. While it is important to pray all the psalms, moving through them on a regular basis so that you become familiar with them, at the beginning it might be easier to flip to the day and choose only one selection. For instance, on Day One, instead of praying all five morning psalms, you could read only one but shift across as the year progresses, Psalm 1 in January, Psalm 2 in February, and so forth.

If you want to keep the BCP monthly or bimonthly cycle but prefer a different translation, then you could consider marking your Bible with M1, E1, M2, E2, for quick reference. (We will further explore the psalms in Chapter Four, page 165.)

Balanced Bible-Reading

Just as we need a balanced prayer life that has ample portions of adoration, confession, thanksgiving, and supplication (ACTS), so our Bible reading needs to be varied and balanced if we are to be healthy Christians.

We all have our favourite passages, for example Psalm 23, the Beatitudes, and the Christmas story, and it is easy just to keep rereading them. But to do so is to shut out the fullness of God. He has far more to reveal.

If you have a basic Christian background, you need to draw daily from both the Old and New Testaments. If you are a seeker looking into the faith or a new convert, it might be simpler to start by reading just a chapter from one New Testament Gospel and a psalm portion each day, before attempting the full Bible. The Gospel of Mark is short and easy to read, and is often suggested first. Others recommend the Gospel of John, which is more mystical and introspective. Matthew and Luke include the Christmas narrative, which Mark and John omit.

An Overview of Salvation

One reason that we see Jesus Christ as the key to salvation is that he fulfils both the law and the prophets. Jesus fulfils the law, in that he obeys perfectly all that God specifies as necessary for holiness, including the Ten Commandments (Exodus 20). Jesus also fulfils the prophets, in that all that was predicted about him centuries earlier came to pass. You can check this out for yourself. After you have read a gospel account of the crucifixion, reread the "Psalm of the Cross," Psalm 22, as well as Psalm 34:20 and Psalm 31:5. Christ's suffering (Passion) is also foretold in Isaiah 52:13 to 53:12. The coming of the Holy Spirit in Acts is foretold in Joel.

These passages provide a brief history of salvation.

Genesis Chapters 1–3	In the beginning, the Creation and the Fall
Exodus Chapters 12–14, 19–20	Passover, Exodus, and Ten Commandments

(cont'd on page 136)

A Brief History of Salvation (cont'd)

Psalms 22, 23, 27, 34, 51, 84, 91, 103, 107, 139	A sampling of ten prayers
Isaiah Chapter 1	Rebellion and forgiveness
Isaiah Chapter 6:1–8	A look into heaven
Isaiah Chapter 40	Comfort for God's people (with shepherd image)
Isaiah Chapter 43:1–13	A Saviour foretold
Isaiah Chapter 52:13–15, 53, 55	The Suffering Servant (Jesus); Promise of Pardon
Joel Chapter 2	The outpouring of the Holy Spirit foretold
A Gospel (Matthew, Mark, Luke, or John)	All about Jesus
Acts Chapters 1–9	The outpouring of the Holy Spirit
Corinthians Chapters 12–13	The gifts of the Spirit; Love
Galatians and Ephesians	The fruit of the Spirit; God's mercy and grace
Revelation Chapters 20–22	The end of the story, heaven opened

This outline is only a kind of short list of salvation, just a very broad sweep. It will help you get started and give you a general framework for understanding God's history of salvation. When we truly commit our lives to Christ, we begin to see how our own personal stories read best within God's story.

The Bible: An Indispensable Library of Books

Christians eventually need to immerse themselves in the full flow of God's Word. But although the river flows from Genesis to Revelation, we can easily get swamped if we simply try to read the Bible from cover to cover, book by book. There are 66 books in the Bible, and they appear in order, according to their subject matter, as if they were on library shelves.

How the Bible is organized:

Old Testament	New Testament
5 books of law*	5 history books
12 history books	(the four Gospels and Acts)
5 poetry books	21 letters
17 books of prophecy	1 book of prophecy set within a letter (Revelation)

(*"Law" is a conventional description. Genesis, Exodus, and Numbers are mostly history, but the oldest statement of Jewish law appears in this group of books, because the law was given in the context of the history.)

There is a risk of getting bogged down if we focus on any one of the shelves. It's better to alternate law with letters, say, or poetry with history. The change in style will be refreshing and more stimulating than reading from one shelf at a stretch.

Remember that we need the *whole* counsel of God. Every
Christian should aim to read through the whole Bible
eventually, and mature Christians should try to reread it
regularly. But if going straight from Genesis to Revelation is not
the most fruitful approach, what approach is better? Many
Christians have found it helpful to use a lectionary.

Lectionaries: Building Variety into Your Bible Reading

A *lectionary* is a system of ordering Scripture passages to be read
in daily or weekly worship. The practice of assigning particular
passages to particular days began in the fourth century, if not
earlier. The lectionaries used in the Book of Common Prayer
have their roots in these ancient times.

The BCP actually provides three interlocking lectionaries or
systems of Bible reading. Taken together, the three lectionaries
are designed to expose worshippers to all the books of Scripture
in a simple and orderly way.

The Eucharistic Lectionary (93–330): The Epistles and Gospels to be read at services of **Holy Communion** on Sundays and holy days are printed in full for the whole church year and take up roughly the second quarter of the Prayer Book. This lectionary, which comes almost intact from the medieval church, highlights key New Testament passages. Usually, it also thematically ties the Epistle with the Gospel, so that one echoes or illuminates the other. The collect, the prayer for the week, often repeats themes from these Scriptures.

The Daily Offices Lectionary: Turn to The Table of Lessons *(xvi),* and you will find the Old and New Testament lessons appointed to be read at services of **Morning** and **Evening Prayer** on every day of the year. This daily lectionary is used by many Anglicans in their private devotions. Unlike systems such as *The One Year Bible,* which is based on the civic calendar year, beginning January 1, it follows the flow of the Church calendar. Different books are pulled off biblical shelves to be read at different times of the year. *Which* book is to be read *when* is harmonized with the church seasons. Isaiah, for example, is read in Advent. This lectionary does not cover every single chapter in the Old Testament. While it presents the whole teaching of Scripture, it avoids the lengthy genealogies and duplications, as well as obscure or easily misunderstood passages. But it faithfully covers every chapter and verse in the New Testament. Several New Testament books are actually read through twice.

The Sunday Offices Lectionary: Embedded within the Table of Lessons *(xvi)* is a separate lectionary for the Sunday services of **Morning** and **Evening Prayer.** This is based on an independent, two-year cycle of reading Scripture. You could think of it as a collection of the "greatest hits of the Bible"! It contains those passages of Scripture that are widely considered to be the most important.

If you are looking for a system of reading Scripture that is less demanding than the full Daily Offices lectionary, you could try using a combination of the Eucharistic lectionary and the Sunday Offices lectionary. This will give you six lessons, keyed both to the Church's year and to the major passages of the Bible, that can be read over the course of each week (one per weekday.)

Don't Play Catch-Up!

Whatever system you use, when you fall behind and miss a few days, don't try to catch up by reading all the missed chapters. Simply plunge in on the current date and move on. Playing catch-up will only discourage you, and you'll throw in the towel. We'll talk more about Scripture on page 170.

Praying the Daily Offices of Morning and Evening Prayer at Home and at Church

Praying Continually: The Origins of the Daily Offices

The psalmist declares, "Seven times a day do I praise thee" (Psalm 119:164). The Apostle Paul urges us to "pray without ceasing" (1 Thessalonians 5:17, KJV). But how is such a thing possible?

For Paul, praying "without ceasing" was not praying *continuously* without interruption every waking moment but *continually*, at frequent intervals, again and again. Mind you, that is still a lot of prayer.

Until its destruction in 70 AD, the Temple at Jerusalem was the site of morning and evening sacrifices according to Jewish law. There were also services of psalms and prayers at 9 a.m. and 3 p.m. Devout Jewish lay people prayed at home in the morning and in the evening as well.

The Jewish practice of regular private prayer was retained by the early Christians. They would meet during the week for morning and evening services that consisted of psalms, canticles, and prayers and, in some places, Scripture-reading and instruction. By the Middle Ages, these services were held in churches and cathedrals, and were becoming increasingly the province of the clergy, although any lay people who were able were still expected to attend them.

These brief weekday services were known as the daily offices. "Office" comes from the Latin *officium,* meaning service or obligation. The daily office was a pattern of worship for Christians to observe each day in their service to God.

At the same time, monasteries and convents were developing more frequent times of prayer—every three hours. By the eighth century in the Western Church, the number of daily offices or services had grown to eight, as follows:

Midnight:	*Matins*	Midday:	*Sext*
3 am	*Lauds*	3 pm	*None*
6 am	*Prime*	6 pm	*Vespers*
9 am	*Tierce*	9 pm	*Compline*

Priests, monks, and nuns were required to pray all eight, while lay people were encouraged to join the monks for two of the daily offices, one in the morning and one in the evening. But many lay people did not live near a cathedral or monastery. Even those who did lacked their own service books and usually could not read or understand Latin. By the eighth century, these services had grown in complexity and were much harder to follow. Later, the reading of Scripture became fragmentary.

Cranmer and Gospel Holiness

In 1549, during the Reformation, the Archbishop of Canterbury, Thomas Cranmer condensed the five huge Latin volumes that guided Roman Catholic worship into one book in English for the reformed Church of England. He streamlined the eight daily offices of the medieval monastery back down to two—our Anglican services of **Morning** and **Evening Prayer**—so that lay people could again easily participate.

Cranmer (1489–1556) took the daily work of prayer out of Latin and put it into English, because he believed in "the priesthood of all believers" (1 Peter 2:9). The parish clergy were called upon to say the daily offices in English in every parish church in the land. Moreover, each church, no matter how small, was required to have a Bible in English, from which the lessons could be read. Cranmer believed holiness involved entering into the Gospel. So he set about providing daily offices at which both clergy and laity could drink deeply from the Bible.

Two additional, shorter offices have been reintroduced in our Canadian Prayer Book: **Prayers for Mid-day** *(16)* and **Compline** *(722)*. As we discussed in the last chapter, these services are provided as options for homes or small groups. But **Morning** and **Evening Prayer** remain the core of regular Anglican daily worship. In this chapter we'll focus mainly on how these services play out in a congregational setting. (Much of what we cover will apply to private worship too.)

Stepping into Prayer Book Worship

Stepping into a BCP service can be a little intimidating at first if you aren't used to this type of worship or are new to church altogether. But don't worry. The Book of Common Prayer works as a script of sorts, enabling us to enter into dialogue with God, a dialogue in which he speaks back to us. We are not passive, silent viewers watching a play. We actively participate throughout the worship.

You may have come from a denomination that only expected the congregation to pray aloud the Lord's Prayer and add *amens* at the end of prayers spoken by others. Of course, by silently praying along and then saying *amen*, you were making those prayers your own. God hears those prayers. That will happen in an Anglican service, too. More often, though, the whole congregation will also pray aloud. Enjoy the quiet thunder of congregational prayer. But don't worry. In a Prayer Book service, you never have to speak alone, except very briefly if you are baptized as an adult, or are confirmed or married.

Congregation, Not Audience

In most Anglican churches, you'll be seated in a pew with other people. You may prefer theatre seating, in which you have your own space on a single chair with arm rests. But there is something to be said, at least symbolically, for six or eight people being stuffed into the same piece of furniture. We speak theologically of being one body in Christ and, for better or worse, you certainly are more together and aware of each other in a pew.

At first glance, you seem to be in the audience. On a raised platform at the front there is a minister who is usually joined by a choir and perhaps some musicians. But despite appearances, you are not the audience watching a performance on stage. You are part of a congregation that is on stage too, along with the minister and musicians. The true audience is God; and, as we will see, he is also the chief actor.

What do we call our worship leaders?

Anglican clergy can be called either "priest" or "minister." The BCP uses both terms interchangeably. Deacons and lay readers may lead **Morning** and **Evening Prayer;** they are also ministers in a sense, but can't properly be called priests.

Embodied Prayer

In Anglican churches, there is usually not only a pew but also a kneeler. Anglicans worshipping according to the Book of Common Prayer kneel for most prayer and stand for praise and psalms, to affirm the creed, and to sing hymns. Sitting is the posture for receiving instruction such as announcements, most Bible lessons, and the sermon. During Communion, Anglicans stand for the reading of the Gospel. Although this is, strictly speaking, a time of instruction, standing is a way of showing respect for Christ, the main actor, as it were, in the Gospel story. Often it is his words that we hear read.

In worship, we present our whole selves to God, body, mind, and spirit, as "living sacrifices, holy and pleasing to God" (Romans 12:1). Prayer with the mouth and not the heart is not prayer. We use embodied prayer, worshipping with mind and mouth, eyes and ears, arms and knees. Some Anglicans will raise their arms in praise, some will make the sign of the cross, but all are expected to kneel in humility and reverence unless they are physically unable to because of disability or age. Don't worry if you feel a little awkward at first. You'll feel less self-conscious with practice.

Flat on Your Face?

In the Bible, there are many occasions when God's people fell prostrate before him with their faces to the ground, such as in Revelation 1:17. Moses and Joshua were told to take off their shoes because they were standing on holy ground, in God's awesome presence (Exodus 3:5; Joshua 5:14, 15). In an Anglican service you will not be expected to fall prostrate or to take off your shoes, but kneeling and bowing your head are other physical ways to express awe in God's presence.

Yet you certainly don't have to hang your head through the whole service. We are told in John 17:1 that "Jesus looked toward heaven and prayed"; so we may too. Looking up is also a well-attested attitude in biblical prayer, just as bowing one's head is. (See John 11:50, Mark 7:34, and Psalm 123:1–2.)

Remember that God is the unseen but very real person you are acknowledging in church and in your private devotions. You are not kneeling or standing out of respect for the priest or the choir or the congregation. They too will kneel before God or stand to honour him. When you pray at home, rather than just slouching in a chair, try to find the space and privacy to kneel and stand.

A Guided Tour of Morning Prayer

We'll spend most of the rest of this chapter looking more closely at the service of **Morning Prayer.** If you open your copy of the BCP and follow along as we discuss each section, you will get a clearer idea of how the service flows. At the end, we'll also take a quick glance at **Evening Prayer,** which has a similar structure. Have a look at the chart below, outlining the two services and the differences between them:

Morning Prayer   **Evening Prayer**

Invitation to worship
Encouragement to confess
Confession and Pardon

(cont'd on page 148)

Morning Prayer	**Evening Prayer** (cont'd)
Lord's Prayer	
Venite	Psalm
Psalm	First Lesson
First Lesson	*Magnificat*
Te Deum	Second Lesson
Second Lesson	*Nunc Dimittis*
Benedictus	
Apostles' Creed	
Collect for the Day	
Collect for Peace	Collect for Peace
Collect for Grace	Collect for Aid against all Perils
Prayers of petition, intercession and thanksgiving	Usually shorter prayers
Prayer of St. Chrysostom	
The Grace	

God Issues an Invitation: A Scriptural Sentence (1)

Remember, God himself invites us to worship him. **Morning Prayer** begins with a sentence from Scripture. St. Matthew and St. Luke, Isaiah and St. Paul were all messengers bearing the invitation, but the message of welcome is God's.

Many of the scriptural sentences speak of the gates of repentance. The very first one is a passage urging confession: "Repent, for the kingdom of heaven is at hand" (Matthew 3:2).

Look at Isaiah 57:15 under "Of Worship" *(3)*, "Thus saith the high and lofty One that inhabiteth eternity, whose name is Holy:

I dwell in the high and holy place, with him also that is of a contrite [repentant] and humble spirit."

Isaiah had several visions of God. He conveys the paradox of God, the holy tension, as it were. God is infinite yet intimate. He is other than us, yet he draws close to us. In theological language, God is both *transcendent* (far above us) and *immanent* (close to us, though invisible). We cannot come face to face with such a holy God and live unless we confess. If we are willing honestly and humbly to pass through the gates of repentance, we are promised God's lavish mercy.

Quite a Jolt: Struck by Holy Lightning

While the actual service of **Morning Prayer** in the Prayer Book begins with an invitation of welcome from God followed by a call to confession, sung church services often open with a powerful hymn of praise. Some people find it a shock to go from standing in joyful adoration of God, belting out choruses of praise, to suddenly falling on their knees in confession. In fact, the juxtaposition is quite biblical. Look at two of the most powerful chapters in the Bible describing worship: Isaiah 6 and Revelation 1.

Isaiah declares, "I saw the Lord seated upon a throne, high and exalted, and the train of his robe filled the temple" (Isaiah 6:1). Angels are calling to one another, 'Holy, Holy, Holy, is the Lord Almighty. The whole earth is full of his glory.'" What is the godly prophet's response to this glorious vision? He feels absolutely wretched! In the Hebrew he speaks of being "cut off," which the King James Version translates as "undone." "Woe to me! I am ruined. For I am a man of unclean lips and I live among a people of unclean lips, and my eyes have seen the King, the Lord Almighty."

Then an amazing thing happens. One of the angels flies to him with a live coal from the fire on the altar. He touches Isaiah's lips and says, "Behold, this has touched your lips; your guilt is taken away and your sin is forgiven" (Isaiah 6:7, RSV). Then Isaiah hears the Lord himself speak, and he replies. Now, cleansed from sin, he can safely remain in the presence and fellowship of the Lord.

Again in the first chapter of Revelation, we see a similar pattern of awe juxtaposed with humility. The author, a man named John, had a vision of heaven in which he saw Christ's face "like the sun shining in all its brilliance." He was so overwhelmed, he fell at Christ's feet "as though dead" (Revelation 1:16–17). We cannot bear such holiness. When we really sense God's glory, we also become more conscious of our own sinfulness.

But hold on, you say. We are in **Morning Prayer,** not heaven. True, but it is in worship that we can sense or glimpse something of heaven. After singing "Holy, Holy, Holy!" or "Praise to the Holiest in the height," it is perhaps not so strange that we should feel the need to fall on our knees and confess. We must seek forgiveness for ourselves and, as Isaiah does, for our world. So we approach our glorious God through the gates of repentance.

A Call to Confess: The Exhortation (4)

Someone has said that we are very good at confessing the sins of others! If only we were so quick to perceive and admit our own faults!

Notice that the first long passage the priest speaks doesn't end with an *amen (4)*. That is because it is not a prayer or cry to God at all but a call to the congregation, both an invitation and a warning. It begins affectionately, "Dearly beloved brethren."

The priest urges us to confess our sins. We want to think the best of ourselves, to overlook our misdeeds or blame others for our faults. Too often we assume we can just stroll up to God as an equal and start talking to him on our terms, as though nothing has happened between us. We forget that when we hurt others, intentionally or otherwise, God is also hurt and offended, because he loves them. We also assume that if we see no faults in ourselves, others see none. That is a mistake.

We cannot fully adore God or thank him or petition him, even for others, or "hear his most holy Word," until we have cleared the air, until we have confessed our failings and been assured of his forgiveness. To get real with God means to let him tell us who we really are. We are sinners, and no matter how good we look to ourselves or to others, our sin has offended God and cut us off from him. It has also damaged us and those around us.

We should not "dissemble nor cloak" our sins "before the face of Almighty God our heavenly Father." Hide-and-seek and dress-up are wonderful children's games. But we cannot hide or disguise our sins from God. After Adam and Eve sinned against God in the garden, they tried to hide from him (Genesis 3:8–10). Don't waste the time. Better to live transparently before him.

sundry:	various, several
manifold:	many
dissemble:	disguise, conceal
penitent:	repentant
sin:	something in us that offends God and keeps us doing things God forbids. (Much sin is caused by the "craft and subtlety of the devil.")
sins:	actual wrong things that we do in thought, word or deed.
repent:	to turn back to God
confess:	to admit the reality of the faults that we have committed
grievous:	causing grief or pain
misdoings:	wrong things we do

Repentance means looking at our lives in the light of God's Word, acknowledging where we have fallen short in our love for God and our neighbour, and where we have gone astray in sinful thoughts, words, and actions. But first and foremost, repentance means turning away from sin and back towards God. It involves admitting that we have done wrong and need God's forgiveness. We are saying, "You know the truth about us, Lord."

Returning to God: A General Confession (4)

So the first prayer we utter in **Morning Prayer** is a prayer of confession. It is called A General Confession *(4)*, because the whole church is confessing openly and in a general manner. These are not specific sins being confessed by one individual privately. During the General Confession priests kneel, too, because they are also confessing their sins.

We say, "We have erred and strayed from thy ways like lost sheep." Jesus called himself the Good Shepherd. When ninety-nine sheep were safe in the fold, Jesus still went looking for the one that was lost and when he found it, carried it safely home on his shoulders. He didn't beat it and drag it home. We are that lost sheep.

When most people think of sin, they think of faults they have committed, the sins of *commission*: "We have done those things which we ought not to have done" *(5)*. But there is another type of sin we often miss: "We have left undone those things which we ought to have done." These are sins of *omission*. They are more hidden, below the radar, as it were, but just as real and dangerous. These are the sins of neglect, the kind words never spoken, the good intentions never acted upon, the evils we tolerate in order to preserve our own position. A child can die from vicious blows, but also from neglect.

"There is no health in us." There is no part of us, mind, will, emotions, or body that is not affected by sin. We are not as bad as we could be, but sin affects every aspect of our nature to some degree. Sin always makes us, at some level, sick. So it is healthy to repent. We are in one sense "miserable sinners," because we are not truly happy or at peace with God until we confess; and even if we don't happen to feel miserable, we are still to be pitied (the older meaning of "miserable"), and we need to throw ourselves on God's compassion.

Some see all this talk of "no health" and "miserable sinners" as going too far. But if you want a spiritual reality check, read Psalm 51. It uses similar words. Nor does the General Confession leave us in the pit of despair. Christ pulls us out. Look at the upward curve: We finish by asking God to "restore" us according to his "promises" so we might live a "godly life" to God's glory.

God Speaks Forgiveness: The Absolution (5)

Remember the coal from the altar that touched Isaiah's lips? Well, we too are going to be absolved, forgiven. God provides the offering, not a coal from a ceremonial fire but the actual sacrifice of his own Son. Jesus is the live coal from the altar. Jesus is both High Priest and Sacrifice.

If we humbly and honestly confess, God will forgive us. We need to hear that forgiveness spoken. To be absolved is to be formally pronounced free from sin, guilt, sentence, or obligation. We are now sinners forgiven. We are pardoned. God declares his favour towards us.

absolution:	setting free from guilt and punishment, declaration of forgiveness
	formal release from guilt, obligation or punishment; acquittal
to absolve:	to acquit; pronounce not guilty; set or pronounce free from blame or obligation
remission:	the debt owed to God for sin is cancelled or literally "sent back"
beseech:	beg, plead
unfeignedly:	truly, not faking it, not pretending

Sins become habits if we keep on committing them, and it is hard for us to break free from such habitual behaviour. Such sin wastes us and leads eventually to spiritual death. But God, in his deep love for us, "desireth not the death of a sinner" but desires "that he may turn from his wickedness and live." God wants life for us. Absolution means being set free. First, God's Holy Spirit convinces us of our sin. He convicts us, but he does not condemn us. Then, when we confess, the same Holy Spirit is given to us as grace to help purify or sanctify us.

God gives his ministers authority to pronounce this absolution and actually commands them to do so. Read the Gospel of John 20:21–23 to see how the Prayer Book agrees with the Bible.

Listen for these key words: "Almighty God ... pardoneth and absolveth all them that truly repent" *(5).*

When We Can't Forgive Ourselves

Sometimes it is hard to recognize our sinfulness. We gloss over it and are in denial. At other times, our sin weighs us down so heavily that we cannot believe that anyone, even God, could ever forgive us. So we need to hear his forgiveness declared loud and clear. We need to accept God's forgiveness. We say we are unworthy. He says that now, through Christ's sacrifice on the cross, he counts us as worthy.

Only a priest can pronounce the Absolution *(5)*, and to make it visibly clear, he stands and faces the congregation. We hear the absolution unmistakably directed towards us. It is from God, and for the priest as well.

In private devotions, in the absence of a priest, it is usual to pray one of the following instead:

"O God, whose nature and property is ever to have mercy …" *(58)*
Collect for 21st Sunday after Trinity *(252)*
Collect for 24th Sunday after Trinity *(257)*
"For Pardon through the Cross" *(730)*

The priest also asks for the Holy Spirit, "We beseech him to grant us … his Holy Spirit." It is not enough to have the evil swept out of our soul. We need God's Spirit to fill the emptiness; to empower us to "please him" now and be "pure and holy" in the future, "so that at the last we may come to his eternal joy." On earth, we are works in progress and will only be perfectly holy in heaven.

You can avoid getting lost in longer prayers such as this one if you listen for key phrases and try to sense the flow of the passage. The Absolution moves from speaking of "the death of a sinner" through "he turns from his wickedness" and "truly repents" to arriving at "eternal joy." So we sense pardon, peace, and hope.

The Gritty Glory of Forgiveness

Forgiveness of sins is one of the most distinctive and glorious aspects of Christianity. Forgiveness is so important that it is a part of the Lord's Prayer and the Apostles' Creed. In the Creed we declare, "I believe in the forgiveness of sins." And in the prayer Jesus taught us, we not only ask to be forgiven, we promise to forgive those who have sinned against us.

Of course, this is all easier said than done. Some days we can hardly mouth, "Forgive those who have trespassed against us," especially when we have suffered great wrongs at the hands of those who do not care. Yet we must forgive others, not because they have apologized (they may never) but because God has forgiven us so much (Matthew 18:21–35) and continues to forgive us.

God is not asking us to deny the very real evil done against us. We need to remember Joseph, whose ten older brothers plotted to murder him, but instead sold him into slavery in Egypt. You can read the whole story in Genesis, Chapters 37 to 50. Joseph had every reason to hate his brothers.

Years later, the tables turn and Joseph is in a position of power in Egypt. He could have had his ten brothers executed or at least let them starve, for a famine had hit their land and only Joseph could supply them and their families with food. The brothers throw themselves at Joseph's feet pleading ironically, "We are your slaves." Joseph answers them with a classic line that both recognizes the very real evil they have done him but also speaks of compassion:

> Fear not, for am I in the place of God? As for you, *you meant evil against me; but God meant it for good,* to bring it about that many people should be kept alive, as they are today.
> (GENESIS 50:19–20, RSV) *[emphasis added]*

Again, on the cross Jesus doesn't pretend that those who are crucifying him have not done him evil, but he forgives them nevertheless: "Father, forgive them, for they know not what they do" (Luke 23:34, KJV). And from that most horrific evil against a total innocent, God is still able to bring the greatest good, the redemption of the world.

Intimacy and Awe: The Lord's Prayer (5)

Our Father who art in heaven. The first line alone captures the paradoxical awe and intimacy we spoke of earlier. We cannot know all there is to know of God, for he is in heaven. He is mysterious and ineffable (too great for any description in words). He is the Other, outside our being and control. Yet his face is turned towards us in fatherly love.

In John's Gospel, Jesus calls God "Father" 122 times, often using the intimate and emphatic *abba.* This Aramaic word is equivalent to "daddy," the expression a young child would use. Yet there is nothing childish about this affectionate address. "Dear father" would be another way of putting it. In the Lord's Prayer, Jesus encourages all his followers to call God, "Father."

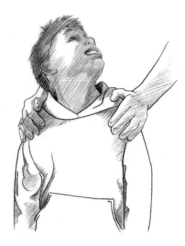

But what if you have only experienced abuse or abandonment from your human father? Can you still pray this prayer? Yes! God doesn't learn how to be a father from our earthly fathers, even from the best of them. Earthly fathers are expected to learn how to parent from God, although some do not. The Bible is realistic about how cruel some fathers and mothers can be, yet God says he will be that perfect Father, and more loving than the most loving earthly mother:

> Can a mother forget the baby at her breast
> and have no compassion on the child she has borne?
> Though she may forget, I will not forget you!
> (ISAIAH 49:15)

The psalmist declares:

> Though my mother and father forsake me,
> the Lord will receive me.
> (PSALM 27:10)

So when we say "Our Father," we may think of the father or mother we never had and always longed for. And we hear our heavenly Father say to us, as Jesus did to those he healed, "my son" or "my daughter" (Mark 2:5, 5:34).

Captured in a Glimpse

Whole books have been written on the Lord's Prayer. One of the finest is *The Prayer that Spans the World,* a series of sermons on the Lord's Prayer delivered in the shattered city of Stuttgart, Germany, during the last days of World War II by Lutheran pastor Helmut Thielicke.[14] In a small book like this, we can capture only a glimpse of this great prayer.

Unpacking the Lord's Prayer

Our Father who art [you who are] in heaven hallowed [sanctified] be thy name	adoration of the Father
thy kingdom come	surrender to his will
thy will be done on earth as it is in heaven	desire for his will
give us this day our daily bread	petition for sustenance for ourselves and others. Note "our."

(cont'd on page 161)

Unpacking the Lord's Prayer *(cont'd)*

forgive us our trespasses as we forgive them that trespass against us	confession recognition of the need for forgiveness in the darkness of the world
lead us not into temptation but deliver us from evil	a cry for deliverance
For thine is the kingdom, the power and the glory for ever and ever,	a burst of praise (a later addition to the original prayer)
Amen.	"So be it." Please make it so.

A Bridge to Praise: Responses and a Doxology (6)

We now have what looks like brief dialogue from a play script, marked minister/people (6). The technical name for these short lines is *suffrages.* (The minister's lines are called *versicles;* the congregation's are called *responses.*) We are entering a section of praise but, as with all prayer, we need God to initiate it. So we ask:

Minister.   O Lord, open thou our lips.
People.   And our mouth shall show forth thy praise.

(PSALM 51:15)

Then come two brief, arrow-like petitions shot straight to heaven:

Minister.   O God, make speed to save us.
People.   O Lord, make haste to help us.

(PSALM 70:1)

God frees us from the prison of our own self-consciousness and gives us a desire to lift our hearts and minds to him, to be God-conscious and God-centred. And praise, as we shall see, expands our consciousness of God as nothing else does.

Here comes another abrupt physical change. We have been down on our knees in humble confession and supplication. Now we stand straight up and glorify God with a burst of praise. The first part is called the *Gloria Patri,* from the first line in Latin "Glory be to the Father." Feel free to get a little louder and more joyous here.

You have just said the shorter or Lesser Doxology. A doxology is a hymn that gives praise to the persons of the Trinity. We will use it again at the end of the psalms. A longer doxology, the *Gloria in Excelsis* or "Glory be to God on high," is used in **Holy Communion** *(86).* Both doxologies are ancient, fourth-century prayers.

Gateway to a Wide Expanse of Praise: The Venite (6)

Stay on your feet, for we are now entering into a wide expanse of praise. We will praise God and then listen to what he says to us. Think of two people in love, how each hangs on every word spoken by the other. This section is a dialogue of love, although sometimes, on God's part, it will be tough love. Sometimes God warns us, but always because he loves us and wants the best for us, an eternity in his embrace. Sometimes, too, especially in the psalms, we will express our frustrations and disappointments and longings to God.

This section of praise and Scripture opens with the *Venite,*
Psalm 95 *(6).* The word *venite,* which means "come," is the first
word of the prayer in Latin. Since the early sixth century, this
psalm has been the call to worship in the first service of corporate
daily prayer in the Western Church. "Let us heartily rejoice,"
that is, rejoice from the heart "in the strength of our salvation."
We have a strong salvation in Christ. "Let us come before his
presence with thanksgiving." Praise and thanksgiving are often
intertwined.

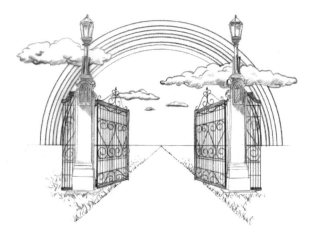

As we praise and honour God, we also yield and surrender to
him. So adoration and commitment go together, just as two
people who love each other also commit and entrust themselves
to one another. "He is the Lord our God, and we are the people
of his pasture and the sheep of his hand."

Sometimes the last four verses beginning "Today, O that ye
would hear his voice ..." can be dropped if time presses. These
darker verses should be heeded, though, because they are a
warning spoken in tough love.

heartily:	from the heart
provocation:	incitement to anger

Hearing God Speak and Replying in Words He Has Given

At first it might seem that we are doing all the talking (and singing). But God talks to us, too. Most of us want to hear God speak personally to us, but we miss the obvious. He has spoken and he continues to speak to us through his Word, the Bible. We need only listen.

The reading of Scripture is the heart of **Morning** and **Evening Prayer.** Three passages are appointed to be read at each service: one from the Book of Psalms, one from the Old Testament—the First Lesson—and one from the New Testament—the Second Lesson. We discussed the Prayer Book's systems of Bible reading in Chapter 3, but just to remind you: the First and Second Lesson for the day are found in the Sunday or Daily Offices lectionary *(xvi–xlvii)*. The psalm or psalms for the day are found by consulting the monthly cycle in the Psalter, or the bimonthly cycle on *page lv.* There is another, third option for selecting the psalms: the table of "Proper Psalms", found on *pages l–liv.* This one contains shorter psalm selections for each Sunday and holy day, and is often used for services of full congregational worship that have been lengthened by the inclusion of hymns, a sermon, and so on.

Praying the Psalms—Even from Prison: The Psalter (331–521)

We can learn much about prayer and praying the psalms from Dietrich Bonhoeffer, a Lutheran pastor and theologian who knelt on the cold prison floor of a Nazi concentration camp:

> ... it is a dangerous error, surely very widespread among Christians, to think that the heart can pray by itself ... Prayer does not mean simply to pour out one's heart. It means rather to find the way to God and to speak to him whether the heart is full or empty. No man can do that by himself. For that he needs Jesus Christ.

> The child learns to speak because his father speaks to him. He learns the speech of his father. So we learn to speak to God because God has spoken to us and speaks to us ... Repeating God's own words after him, we begin to pray to him ... The words that come from God become, then, the steps on which we find our way to God ...[15]

God speaks to us through the psalms and we can speak back to him using the very words he has given us.

The Psalter has nourished the spirituality of more Christians than any other book in the Old Testament. St. Benedict (480–550), the founder of the Benedictine monastic order, made it a requirement of his Rule that the whole Psalter should be said or sung each week in monasteries and convents. As we said in the previous chapter, the Book of Common Prayer also values the regular praying of the Psalter but stretches it over a month, or even two months, to make it more manageable, especially for lay people.

All our emotions and situations, and the hopes and fears of those we are interceding for, find full expression in the psalms *(331–521)*.

Sometimes the psalm appointed for the day fits our soul's mood perfectly. We come to worship joyful or thankful, and the psalm chosen expands our joy and gratitude. Other days we come burdened with sorrow, and the psalm is appropriately a lament.

Out of Whack: Appointed, But Not Appropriate?

But the psalm or psalms appointed can be out of whack with how we feel spiritually. How can we pray a lament when we are joyful or give thanks when we're desperately ill? Certainly, in corporate worship, no psalm will suit everyone.

As Christians, we are called into community. If you are in church, look around you. You are in the midst of a praying community. Pray with them. You are rejoicing, but who is grieving? Lament with them. You are sorrowing, but who is bursting with joy? This can be hard, but try to rejoice with them. St. Paul tells us to "Rejoice with those who rejoice; mourn with those who mourn" (Romans 12:15). Praying the appointed psalm helps to make that possible.

So an appointed psalm that doesn't match your mood at a particular moment may fit the needs of someone you could be praying for. Even in private devotions, it is a good spiritual discipline to pray the psalms *seriatim,* (in order) and thus use them to intercede for others.

Handling Hate with Care

The psalms express the whole sweep of human emotions, including hate. There are more than two dozen psalms that contain curses against enemies. Yet even if these cursing psalms express righteous anger against real evil, should we pray them? After all, Jesus taught, "Love your enemies and pray for those who persecute you" (Matthew 5:44).

Let's look at the most disturbing curse, the one found in Psalm 137. The Israelites have been taken into captivity, dragged from Jerusalem to Babylon. They have suffered many atrocities. In the first six verses they lament their desolation, "By the waters of Babylon we sat down and wept ..." Then in the last three verses they utter a vicious curse, perhaps hoping to inflict on the Babylonians what they themselves have suffered:

> O Daughter of Babylon, doomed to destruction, happy is he who repays you for what you have done to us — who seizes your infants and dashes them against the rocks.
>
> (PSALM 137:8–9)

No statement in the psalms is more brutal. But at least it is honest. When we experience evil first hand or when we see an innocent person abused, our gut reaction is to strike back. But the psalmist doesn't take personal revenge. He asks God to bring down judgement. He cries out to God for justice; he doesn't attack the oppressor himself.

To turn a blind eye to abuse, torture, or massacre is to condone it. That would be moral indifference that is deadly for our souls.

Caring for Both Victim and Oppressor

It has been said that hate for the oppressor is the first sign that we care for the victim.[16] When we curse those who exploit and oppress the vulnerable and innocent, we are praying for justice. We may have been the one wronged. Or our anger may be aroused when we see another victimized. God cares for the soul of both the victim and the oppressor, so we must too.

God can handle every emotion we bring to him, even hate. Our anger, whether righteous or not, needs to be prayed through, not suppressed. Then God can deal with it. We need to open up our deepest wounds to God's healing touch. Otherwise, they will only fester.

Miroslav Volf, a Croatian theologian, suffered a great deal during the war in the 1990s in the former Yugoslavia. He writes, "We place both our unjust enemy and our own vengeful self face to face with a God who loves and does justice." He explains that hate that hides away from God grows in the darkness and infests everything. "In the light of justice and love of God, however, hate recedes and the seed is planted for the miracle of forgiveness."[17]

All biblical cries for God to avenge evil need to be handled with great care. They can so easily be misunderstood and taken out of context. Because of this, the cursing passages in the psalms are rarely heard in worship services. The most severe were omitted from the 1962 version of the Canadian BCP. A note on *page xlix* lists these passages.

The Innocent Child Struck against the Rock

Dietrich Bonhoeffer gives us another take on the cursing psalms, reminding us that the evils against which the psalmists railed were often recognized by the Israelites as brought down upon themselves through their own disobedience. He writes,

> The enemies referred to here [in the psalms] are enemies of the cause of God, who lay hands on us for the sake of God. It is nowhere a matter of personal conflict … I myself, with my sin, belong under this judgement …

> God's vengeance did not strike the sinners, but the one
> sinless man who stood in the sinner's place, namely
> God's own Son. Jesus Christ bore the wrath of God for
> the execution of which the psalm prays. He stilled
> God's wrath towards sin and prayed in the hour of the
> execution of the divine judgement, "Father, forgive
> them, for they know not what they do!"... That is the
> end of all the phony thoughts about the love of God
> which does not take sin seriously.[18]

So whose child is struck against the rock? God's own innocent
Son, and for our sake, and the sake of all sinners, including Nazis
and ancient Babylonians, while we were yet enemies of God.
Bonhoeffer turns upside down the cry for vengeance against
those who do us evil.

Bonhoeffer knew real enemies. He returned to Germany at the
beginning of World War II. First, he was forbidden to teach.
Then he was imprisoned for two years. Finally, on April 9, 1945,
only a month before the war in Europe ended, he was hanged.
Yet he could write while imprisoned, "I cannot forgive the enemies of God out of my own resources. Only the crucified Christ
can do that, and I through him."[19]

Listen Up! The First (Old Testament) Lesson (7)

In the first lesson, we hear from the Old Testament. This reading
could be law, history, poetry, or prophecy. Some passages can be
quite dramatic.

When we hear Scripture read in church or read it privately
ourselves, we need to respond like little Samuel in the temple.
We need to say to God in our hearts, "Speak, for thy servant
heareth" (1 Samuel 3:10, KJV). We need to listen up. Moses tells

the Israelites, "They are not just idle words for you—they are your life" (Deuteronomy 32:47). Read and listen expectantly. Trust that through his own Word, God is going to speak to you.

News Report or Editorial?

God speaks to us in different styles on different pages of the Bible.

When you read about an accident or crime on the front page of a newspaper, you learn, often in gruesome detail, what happened. But the reporter doesn't tell you in the news report how upsetting it was to have to cover the story. The reporter may well have cried at the scene of the horror. The editor may have felt sick while editing the report. Just because they don't comment on page one about how awful they felt, doesn't mean that they are glad that the accident or crime happened. Opinions on events are usually saved for the editorial pages and for opinion columns.

In the Bible, too, especially in the Old Testament, events are sometimes told without any immediate commentary. Some biblical history is written with no adjacent "editorial comment" as it were, from God. Sometimes, people make the mistake of thinking that if an event was recorded in the Bible without immediate commentary, then God was glad it happened. But that would be like saying that the reporter and editor were glad that the accidents and crimes recorded on the front page happened. We have to turn to the editorial pages to see what the editors or columnists think and feel about the recorded events of the day.

So when you read of some particularly distressing event in the Bible, you may need to turn to another section to learn how God feels about it. That's one reason we need to read the whole Bible to get the whole picture, just as we need to read both the front page and the editorial pages of a newspaper, if we want the whole story.

Sound Bite or Lifelong Conversation?

We, of course, often want only a brief sound bite from God—twenty-five words or less. We want him to speak quickly to us and tell us what to do, but we don't really want to "waste" any time listening at length. We would never expect a good parent or a fine teacher to impart all their wisdom in sixty seconds. Yet people foolishly open the Bible and think that God will tell them all they need to know in the first one or two verses they chance upon.

There is a rather dark joke about the man who wanted to discover God's will for his life, and so he opened up his Bible. But instead of reading as much as he could, he planned to read and obey only the first verse he set eyes upon, which unfortunately was, "Judas … went away and hanged himself" (Matthew 27:5). The joke continues that the man then thought he would try another verse so he haphazardly flipped to the end of Luke 10:37, "Go and do likewise."

Those who have read further in the Bible know that God is a God of hope who does not want people to despair and commit suicide. He provides tremendous grace, often in the midst of dire circumstances, but we have to read far more than two random verses to learn this. We need a personal relationship with God, and meaningful relationships involve long conversations over many months, not sixty-second sound bites.

God-Breathed

Many of us are biblically illiterate. We need to ask the Holy Spirit to be our teacher or tutor, interpreting the passage for us. The words are not just dead letters on the page or sounds echoing in a building. They are God-breathed. Jesus said, "The words that I have spoken to you are spirit and life" (John 6:63b, RSV).

Be ready to let Scripture search and accuse you, comfort and heal you. Is there a sin to avoid or confess? Is there an example or command to follow? Is there a promise to claim, a gift to receive or give thanks for? What more does this passage reveal about God as I try to trust him? Often it helps to imagine that you are one of the people in the story. It gets you more deeply into what is going on.

Even great biblical scholars admit that they do not perfectly understand everything in the Bible. John Stott, a British Anglican theologian, encourages us to "grapple with," not ignore the problems. "And as we study them, some will diminish or even disappear (many problems that troubled former generations are no longer problems today). Yet some problems will remain."[20]

We pray for God to enlighten us about what still puzzles us. But we should try to obey what we do understand. We should not be like the lazy student who told his teacher, "I didn't understand the last of the twenty questions in my assignment, so I didn't do any of my homework." No teacher would accept that. Obey what you understand and pray for guidance in what you don't.

Even when we understand perfectly well what a passage means with our heads, it is often hard to obey it in our hearts. We need to pray for understanding *and* obedience:

> Blessed Lord, who hast caused all holy Scriptures to be written for our learning: Grant that we may in such wise hear them, read, mark, learn, and inwardly digest them, that by patience and comfort of thy holy Word, we may embrace and ever hold fast the blessed hope of everlasting life, which thou hast given us in our Saviour Jesus Christ. *Amen.*
>
> *Second Sunday in Advent (97)*

All You Need to Know—For Your Salvation

We will never understand the whole mind of God, simply because we are not God. The Bible, however, tells us all that we need to know for our salvation. It is the textbook for our souls and teaches us all the essentials we need to learn for our redemption, for a restored relationship with God.

The BCP explains in the Anglican Articles of Religion *(698–714):*

> Holy Scripture containeth all things necessary to salvation: so that whatsoever is not read therein, nor may be proved thereby, is not to be required of any man, that it should be believed as an article of the Faith, or be thought requisite [required] or necessary to salvation.
>
> *Article VI "Of the Sufficiency of Scripture" (700)*

Q & A

The importance of Scripture is stated in a question and answer format in **A Supplementary Instruction to the Catechism** *(552):*

Question: *Why ought you to read God's holy Word, the Bible?*

Because it tells how God has made himself known to man; and how we may come to know him, and find salvation through our Lord Jesus Christ in the fellowship of his Church.

Question: *What does the Church teach about the Bible?*

The Bible records the Word of God as it was given to Israel, and to his Church, at sundry [various] times and in divers [different] manners; and nothing may be taught in the Church as necessary to man's salvation unless it be concluded or proved therefrom.

Question: *Where then is the Word of God to be found in all its fullness?*

In Jesus Christ, his only Son, who was made man for us and for our salvation. *(554–555)*

Hearing God Speak in Stereo

Now, if Jesus is the fullness of the Word of God, do Christians need to bother reading the Old Testament? Yes.

Once, when Jesus quoted a psalm he said, "the Scripture cannot be broken" (John 10:34). Again he proclaimed during the Sermon on the Mount:

> Do not think that I have come to abolish the Law or the Prophets; I have not come to abolish them but to fulfil them. I tell you the truth, until heaven and earth disappear, not the smallest letter, not the least stroke of a pen, will by any means disappear from the Law until everything is accomplished.
>
> (MATTHEW 5:17–18)

Jesus said to his disciples after his resurrection:

> "Everything must be fulfilled that is written about me in the Law of Moses, the Prophets and the Psalms." Then he opened their minds so they could understand the Scriptures.
>
> (LUKE 24:44)

Of course, the Scriptures that are referred to here are not the New Testament—it hadn't been written then—but the Old Testament.

Like the writers of the Old Testament books, these first-century disciples would need a special outpouring of the Holy Spirit to write the New Testament documents. Before his death, Jesus said to his disciples, "But the Counsellor, the Holy Spirit, whom the Father will send in my name, will teach you all things and will remind you of everything I have said to you" (John 14:26).

But there is a sense in which we, too, as Jesus' followers in the twenty-first century, also receive the Holy Spirit to be our teacher or tutor, to open our minds to understand the Scriptures. We need to hear God speak to us from both Old and New Testaments because the one informs the other. It has been said that the New Testament has been hidden in the Old, and the Old becomes visible in the New.

The Bible Jesus Read

Jesus quoted often from the Old Testament and never from any other book. In *The Bible Jesus Read,* American journalist Philip Yancey writes, "When we read the Old Testament, we read the Bible Jesus read and used."[21] Article VII of the Anglican Articles of Religion spells out the interrelationship between the Old and New Testaments:

> The Old Testament is not contrary to the New: for both
> in the Old and New Testament everlasting life is offered
> to Mankind by Christ, who is the only Mediator
> between God and Man, being both God and Man.
> *Article VII "Of the Old Testament" (701)*

Article VII goes on to explain that the law given from God by Moses concerning ceremonies and rites is not binding on Christians, yet every Christian is to obey the moral commandments of the Old Testament. In other words, as the Epistle to the Hebrews says, the laws in the Old Testament that describe sacrifices required for sin and purification from uncleanness have been brought to completion with the coming of Christ. But still we are bound to obey the moral law, which Jesus himself underlined and reiterated (Matthew 5:17–48).

"Of the whole of the Scripture there are two parts: the law and the gospel," said Philip Melanchthon (1497–1560), a German Reformer. "The law indicates the sickness, the gospel the remedy."

The Old Testament is three-quarters of the Bible, and contains thirty-nine books written over a millennium by several dozen authors. It records God's gradual revelation of himself and his ways to his chosen servants and prophets, a process that was only completed in his begotten Son and living Word, Jesus Christ. You can find an explanation and summary of this in the first chapter of the Epistle to the Hebrews.

The Third World often understands the Old Testament better than the developed world. Those in Africa and parts of Asia easily grasp stories of tribal feuds, land disputes, arranged marriages, water rights, and ancestral worship, because they are still challenges of everyday life.

We cannot fully understand the New Testament without the Old. The Epistle to the Hebrews, the Epistle of Jude, and the book of Revelation are particularly dependent on the Old Testament. The Gospels can be read as "stand-alones," but you will miss much of their richness. Images such as the Lamb of God, the Good Shepherd, the Sign of Jonah, the anointed king, and the Suffering Servant all make more sense if we know their Old Testament context.

Many people, including philosopher Justin Martyr (*c.*100–165) and French mathematician, physicist, and philosopher, Blaise Pascal (1623–1662), came to faith when they realized how Jesus dramatically fulfills Old Testament prophecy.

Let's go back to **Morning Prayer.** God speaks to us through the Old Testament Lesson. Now we stand to reply in praise.

Singing, Even Without a Tune: The Te Deum *(7)*

As we learned in Chapter One, a canticle is a song of praise, often taken from the Bible, but not usually from the Book of Psalms. These ancient hymns are called by their Latin names, which are their first words in Latin.

Te Deum Laudamus, "We praise thee, O God" is often just called the *Te Deum* from its opening words in Latin, which mean "thee, O God." It has long been acknowledged as one of the most magnificent of the ancient hymns of the Church. Certain scholars believe it was written in 414 AD by Bishop Niceta of Nish, which is in the former Yugoslavia. So it has probably been prayed for nearly 1600 years.

You can identify its three sections from the large print of their first words: We/Thou/O Lord. When you pray the *Te Deum*, you suddenly realize that you are not praying alone to God. You are joining a huge throng of worshippers.

Who are the worshippers in the *Te Deum?*

all the earth
all angels
the heavens and all the powers therein
the Cherubim and Seraphim (two orders of angels)
the Apostles
the Prophets
the Martyrs (those killed for their faith)
the holy Church throughout all the world

If we are known by the company we keep, this is good company to be in! May their ardent devotion rub off on us. We echo and repeat the song of the angels in heaven itself, an eternal hymn that Isaiah heard and told us of:

Holy, Holy, Holy, Lord God of Hosts,
Heaven and earth are full of the majesty of thy glory.

(ADAPTED FROM ISAIAH 6:3)

By the end of the first section, glory and honour are given to the three persons of the Trinity.

The first section of the *Te Deum* unpacked:

We ... acknowledge thee, the Father of an infinite Majesty	God has royal, divine dignity, yet he is also our Father.
Thine honourable, true, and only Son	The Son is worthy of all honour.
Also the Holy Ghost, the Comforter	*Ghost* means "spirit," from the Old English *gast*. *Comforter* means "strengthener, one who comes alongside to befriend and advise."

The second section begins, "Thou art the King of Glory, O Christ" and builds, "Thou art the everlasting Son of the Father." What follows is rather like a more poetic version of the Apostles' Creed. Let's compare the *Te Deum*, particularly this second section, with the Apostles' Creed *(10)*. While the duplication is not exact, the parallels are striking, as the box on pages 182 and 183 shows:

The *Te Deum* (7)	The Apostles' Creed *(10)*
(selections)	*(the whole creed)*

We acknowledge thee to be the Lord ... I believe in God

The Father of an infinite Majesty — the Father Almighty

all the earth doth worship thee ... — Maker of heaven and
heaven and earth are full of — earth
   thy glory.

Thine honourable, true and only Son — And in Jesus Christ
       his only Son our Lord

Thou art the King of Glory, O Christ.
Thou art the everlasting Son of
   the Father.

When thou tookest upon thee — Who was conceived by
   to deliver man —   the Holy Ghost
thou didst not abhor the Virgin's womb — Born of the Virgin Mary

When thou hadst overcome the — Suffered under Pontius
   sharpness of death —   Pilate
   Was crucified, dead,
      and buried
   He descended into hell

Thou didst open the kingdom — The third day he rose
   of heaven to all believers —   again from the dead
   He ascended into heaven

(cont'd on page 183)

The Te Deum, *The Apostles' Creed* (cont'd)

Thou sittest at the right hand of God in the glory of the Father.	And sitteth on the right hand of God, the Father Almighty
We believe that thou shalt come to be our Judge	From thence he shall come to judge the quick [living] and the dead
[We acknowledge] Also the Holy Ghost the Comforter [out of sequence; appears earlier]	I believe in the Holy Ghost
We therefore pray thee help thy servants, whom thou hast redeemed with thy precious blood.	The holy Catholic Church
Make them to be numbered with thy Saints	The Communion of Saints
O Lord, have mercy upon us, have mercy upon us [appears later]	The Forgiveness of sins
	The Resurrection of the body
in glory everlasting [appears earlier]	And the Life everlasting,
Our trust is in thee ... in thee have I trusted let me never be confounded.	*Amen.*

The third section of the *Te Deum* is a later addition to the original hymn and is sometimes omitted. There is still a note of praise in two lines; see if you can find them. The rest is petition and commitment, echoing the psalms. In the last line, especially, we surrender ourselves to God's mercy and commit our lives to him, "O Lord, in thee have I trusted: let me never be confounded."

Winds, Wells, and Whales: Benedicite, Omnia Opera *(26)*

During Advent and Lent and on certain other days, the *Te Deum* is replaced with the *Benedicite, Omnia Opera (26).* Don't worry. We are not squeezing an opera into our worship, although this is certainly the longest of the canticles. The English title is "O, All ye works of the Lord, Bless ye the Lord." *Opera* is Latin for "works." And the cast praising God, all his works, is huge, his whole creation including fire and heat, dews and frosts, ice and snow, wind, wells and whales, all fowls of the air, all beasts and cattle. "What next?" you may ask.

This is a wonderful canticle for our environmentally conscious age. Christians do not worship creation; instead they join the rest of God's creation in glorifying him. In the midst of a snowstorm, it always seems appropriate to sing "Frost and cold, ice and snow, bless ye the Lord." But according to the biblical story with which the *Benedicite* is associated, it was first sung in a furnace!

The *Benedicite* is also known as the "Song of the Three Children," and you can find their names in the last verse: Ananias, Azarias, and Misael. These youths also have Babylonian names: Shadrach, Meshach, and Abednego. Nebuchadnezzar, the arrogant king of Babylon, threw them into a fiery furnace when they refused to worship a golden idol he had made. You can read their story in the Old Testament in the first three chapters of Daniel. God preserves them and they come out alive, but this song is attributed to them in the midst of the flames.

(*Note:* To shorten the *Benedicite*, you can repeat the refrain, "praise him, and magnify him for ever" only at the end of a group of three verses, or at the end of a section, instead of after each verse.)

The Second (New Testament) Lesson (9)

Now comes the second lesson. This is drawn from the New Testament, from the days when Jesus walked on earth (and water) and from the infancy of the Church. Four different writers, Matthew, Mark, Luke, and John, each have a different take on Jesus. From them we hear Christ's actual words and the stories he told (parables) as well as the things that he did. These are called the Gospels, meaning "good news." After them comes a book called "The Acts of the Apostles." Some people think of it as "The Acts of the Holy Spirit," because it shows how the Holy Spirit empowered the disciples to act in ways that were faithful to Christ after his death and resurrection. Following that are letters sent by various disciples to the newly formed churches, as well as to a few individuals. Finally there is a prophecy known as Revelation, in which we are given a vision of heaven opened and the end of this world.

The Gospel Truth?

Do people always believe the Gospels when they read them for the first time? Should we expect them to? No, it may take longer for some. Consider the advice of Anglican theologian John Stott:

> We should come to the Gospels (which tell the story of Jesus) without any doctrine of Scripture or theory of inspiration at all. We are content merely to take them at their face value as first-century documents (which they are) recording the impressions of eye-witnesses. Next, as we read the Gospels, their testimony, (through the work of the Holy Spirit) leads us to faith in Jesus as Lord. And then this Lord Jesus gives us a doctrine of Scripture, (his own doctrine, in fact), which we did not have at the beginning …
>
> The central issue is not the authority of the Bible but the authority of Jesus. If he accepted the Old Testament as God's Word, are we going to reject it? If he appointed and authorized his apostles, saying to them, "he who receives you receives me," are we going to reject them? To reject the authority of either the Old Testament or the New Testament is to reject the authority of Christ. It is supremely because we are determined to submit to the authority of Jesus Christ as Lord that we submit to the authority of Scripture.[22]

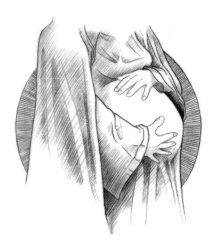

The Song of a Man Struck Dumb: The **Benedictus** *(9)*

If singing isn't your thing, you may find canticles hard to take. Of course, you can say them in your private devotions. If you weren't blessed with a good voice, take comfort from this third canticle, the *Benedictus,* which is Latin for "Blessed." It was first sung by Zachariah, a priest to whom God had sent his angel Gabriel to announce that he and his wife Elizabeth would have a son. But because he and Elizabeth were both elderly, Zachariah doubted God. The angel struck him dumb until his son was born. Then, filled with the Holy Spirit, he proclaimed God's "mighty salvation" and "tender mercy."

?

Benedictus "Mystery Person" Quiz

David and Abraham are honoured in the first section of the *Benedictus*. Two more people are proclaimed in the second section, but not by name. Can you guess their identities from the italicized text?

1. And thou, child, shalt be called the *Prophet of the Highest:* for thou shalt go before the face of the Lord to prepare his ways;
   To give knowledge of salvation unto his people for the remission of their sins.

2. Through the tender mercy of our God; whereby *the day-spring from on high* hath visited us;
   To give light to them that sit in darkness and in the shadow of death, and to guide our feet into the way of peace.

The first, "the Prophet of the Highest," is Zachariah and Elizabeth's son, John the Baptist, who will prepare the way for Christ, by preaching repentance for the forgiveness of sins. The second, "the day-spring from on high," is Jesus, God's own Son, who will, as the Messiah, rescue those lost in darkness and in the shadow of death. You can read the birth stories of these two boys, who are both heralded by the angel Gabriel, in the first chapter of Luke. Then in Chapter 3, John and Jesus meet again as men in their early thirties for a significant event.

A Geography of Joy—Alternative Canticles

Jubilate Deo (457)	Psalm 100
Cantate Domino, "Sing unto the Lord" *(28)*	Isaiah 42:10–12
Surge, Illuminare, "Arise, shine" *(28)*	Isaiah, 60:1–3, 11, 18–19

Alternatives are provided to all of the canticles to prevent worship from getting dull. Instead of the *Benedictus*, we can say the brief *Jubilate Deo*. The Latin title alone seems buoyant with joy and translates as "O be joyful in the Lord." From the same Latin root, we get "jubilation." This four-verse canticle urges us to "serve the Lord with gladness, and come before his presence with a song." Why? Because "the Lord is gracious, his mercy is everlasting."

Two more alternative canticles can serve as sheer bursts of joy in **Morning** or **Evening Prayer.** Both are songs of the prophet Isaiah. *Cantate Domino* is a geography of joy. No matter where you presently live, even if you inhabit the ends of the earth, you are invited to "Sing unto the Lord a new song."

Surge, Illuminare has a startling light metaphor that surges through the whole piece. This Old Testament prophecy foretells the eternal city which we will one day inhabit. We can read more about this new Jerusalem in the last two chapters of the Bible (Revelation 21 and 22). This canticle is especially appropriate for Advent, when we think about Jesus' promised return, and the weeks after Epiphany, which celebrate his coming as the Saviour of all.

Who Do You Say I Am? The Apostles' Creed (10)

Now we go on to say the Apostles' Creed. The Prayer Book contains three creeds, from the word *credo*, "I believe." The Apostles' Creed is the shortest of the three creeds that were adopted in ancient times by the Western Church. It is said at both **Morning** and **Evening Prayer** *(10, 22)* and at **Baptism** *(526, 535)*. The longer Nicene Creed is said at **Holy Communion** *(71)*. The longest of the three, the Creed of St. Athanasius *(695)*, is sometimes proclaimed on Trinity Sunday or in Christmastide or Eastertide. It contains the most detailed teaching on the Trinity and the Incarnation.

"Who do people say the Son of Man is?" Jesus asked his disciples. They knew all the confused thinking, all the mistaken notions people had. At the best, the crowds thought Jesus was a prophet. Then Jesus asks his disciples. "Who do *you* say I am?" This is the really important question. Peter answers, "You are the Christ, the Son of the living God" (Matthew 16:13–16). Today people still have all sorts of mistaken notions about Jesus. Some think he was a liar or a madman. Some think he was a good teacher or a great prophet, but they don't believe he is God. Jesus asks us, despite what the world thinks, "Who do *you* say that I am?"

When we stand to proclaim our faith in the words of the Apostles' Creed, we are answering Christ himself. We are putting our seal on the lessons just read.

The Creed summarizes our faith by stating the essentials. Almost all Christian denominations affirm the Apostles' Creed. Different Christians may disagree on many secondary matters, but on these core issues they almost universally agree.

The Apostles' Creed falls into three sections: God the Father, Jesus Christ, and the Holy Spirit. Let's start with the middle section.

Just a Good Teacher?

Many people think of Jesus as just a good teacher who led an exemplary life, but not as the holy Son of God. They believe he might have performed some miracles but they don't believe the greatest miracle of all, which is that he rose from the dead. The Apostles' Creed *(10)* and the Nicene Creed *(71)* start by affirming Jesus' birth of a virgin (the Incarnation), then jump right over all his teachings, healings, and other miracles, passing straight to his suffering, death, and Resurrection. (The *Te Deum* skips over his ministry too.) When Christians affirm these two creeds, they still believe that Jesus is a great teacher, healer, and miracle-worker but that his birth, death, and Resurrection are the most telling facts of his life. They believe that Jesus is not just a good human teacher but that he is who he claimed to be, fully human and fully divine, perfect man and perfect God,

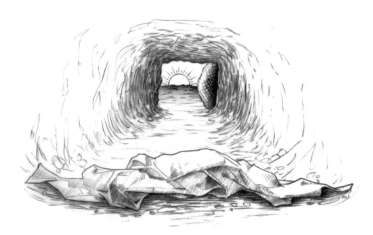

To confess is to acknowledge. We have earlier acknowledged our sins. We should be ashamed of our sins. In the Creed, we confess the essentials of our faith. We are not ashamed of them. We are acknowledging certain key facts, avowing them, affirming them. It is rather like swearing a solemn oath.

Even though we are speaking together aloud, we do not say "We believe" but "I believe." It is important for us each personally to make this acknowledgement. This is not just our parents' faith or our community's faith; it is our own faith. Peter was asked individually, and so are we, "Who do you say that I am?" Despite what we may have been through this week, despite what the world may say about our faith, we now each affirm "I believe in God the Father Almighty, ... in Jesus Christ his only Son our Lord, ... in the Holy Ghost"—the three persons of the Trinity.

To believe the Creed doesn't mean that you fully understand it. We are not God. Much in the Christian faith is a mystery, but to say "I believe in God ..." is also to say "I trust" in this God. We identify with him who has identified himself with us.

The Apostles' Creed is a statement of faith used in the Western Church. Despite its name, it was not composed by the Apostles, but evolved from a creed used in Rome in the second century. It summarizes the faith of the apostles, as taught in the New Testament, and professed by new converts at baptism. It has remained the baptismal creed ever since, and it secured a place in the daily offices between the seventh and ninth centuries.

Puzzled?

One phrase that is often misunderstood is "He [Jesus] descended into hell." In the **Baptism** services *(526, 535)* and the **Catechism** *(545)*, an explanatory note is added to the Creed, saying that this means, "He went into the place of departed spirits," which was sometimes called "hell," without necessarily implying a place of punishment. The point that the Creed wants to stress is that he really did die. If he only "seemed" to die, then what followed was merely a resuscitation, not a glorious resurrection.

The "holy Catholic Church" means the whole or universal Church, not any one denomination. The BCP teaches that the Church is called Catholic "Because it is universal, it holds for all time, in all countries, and for all people, the whole truth as it is in Jesus Christ, who is the same yesterday, today and forever" (**A Supplementary Instruction,** *page 553*).

"Holy Ghost" means Holy Spirit; as we said, the original meaning of "ghost" was "spirit." Only later did the word "ghost" come to be identified with Halloween spooks. "The quick and the dead" means the living and the dead; "quick" originally meant "living."

A lot is packed into these fifteen lines. If you still don't feel you understand what the Creed means, or do not believe what it says, you should keep listening patiently and prayerfully to the section you do not grasp and ask God to teach you. You might want to read a book on the subject by a respected author, for example, Alister McGrath's *I Believe: Understanding and Applying the Apostles' Creed*.[23] We'll talk more about asking questions under I Don't Get It??!! on page 210. A good prayer for situations in which we only partly understand something is, "Lord, I believe. Help thou mine unbelief" (Mark 9:24, KJV).

Asking with Confidence

This is how big my God is as I've seen him revealed by praise and by his Word in Scripture and as I've declared him to be by reciting the Creed. Now I can confidently ask him for my own needs and the needs of others, and after that thank him for what he has already done for us.

Mutual Salutation: Responses (10)

These short arrow prayers break into what has been a long stretch of psalms, canticles, Bible readings, and Creed. They alert us to a change coming, for they serve as a bridge into the prayers of supplication and thanksgiving with which the service will close.

First, there is a lovely mutual salutation or spiritual greeting between the minister and the people, "The Lord be with you"/"And with thy spirit." For a moment we are not speaking to God but to each other under God's gaze. It is drawn from the greeting Boaz gives his reapers (among them his future bride,

Ruth), which you can read in Ruth 2:4. Then the minister invites us again to pray.

Now kneeling, we utter, "Lord have mercy upon us/Christ have mercy upon us/Lord have mercy upon us." This Lesser Litany is in a Trinitarian form. The first appeal is made to the Lord, our Father, the second appeal to the Lord Christ and the third to the Lord, the Holy Spirit. Are we going back to confession? Yes and no. This should be our normal stance before God, because we live as sinners forgiven. It expresses an attitude of humility or deep reverence before God, as we continually seek his mercy. Dr. Robert Crouse, an eminent Canadian Anglican theologian, calls this attitude "penitential adoration."[24]

The Second Our Father (11)

Before we go any further into petition, we now say the "Our Father" again. This may strike you as odd and even redundant. Isn't once enough? Yet this prayer is the pattern Christ himself gave us and upon which we should model all our worship. The Book of Common Prayer makes significant and frequent use of the Lord's Prayer. It stands at the head of many sequences of prayer in the BCP, as a means of putting what follows into perspective. At the beginning of this service it led us into joyful praise. Here it leads us into humble petition. We come to appreciate its richness in these different settings. And our prayerfulness gains intensity through its repetition.

Petition: Shooting More Arrow Prayers

The next set of responses is also lifted mostly from the psalms. We begin to petition for others as well as ourselves. The petition for the Queen is for both her spiritual salvation and her defence on this earth. It is not only for her but also for all those who govern us. When we pray, "Endue thy Ministers with righteousness," we are referring not to our political ministers but to the clergy who minister to us.

Perhaps we could exclaim, "Make thy chosen people joyful" with some burst of joy. Too often this is uttered with all the delight of a dirge. Some have said that it seems to be the one petition God has not answered, for we sound so miserable. "Give peace in our time, O Lord" can be prayed not only for our own nation but also for a just peace in the world. We might name under our breath some trouble spots in the world. "Evermore mightily defend us" can refer to both political and spiritual realities. Often we can pray on several levels at once. The responses close with a petition for purity from Psalm 51:10, 11.

Collect for the Day

We discussed collects earlier on page 105. Let's just look at one now:

> O God, the protector of all that put their trust in thee, without whom nothing is strong, nothing is holy: Increase and multiply upon us thy mercy; that, thou being our ruler and guide, we may so pass through things temporal, that we finally lose not the things eternal. Grant this, O heavenly Father, for Jesus Christ's sake our Lord. *Amen.*
>
> *Fourth Sunday after Trinity (223)*

Powerful Prayers for Protection (11)

Next come two collects that never change. One is the Collect for Peace and the other for Grace, although both pray for God's protection. "Defend us … in all assaults of our enemies, that we, surely trusting in thy defence, may not fear the power of any adversaries" and "Defend us … with thy mighty power" from "sin" and "danger." These are powerful prayers of protection in both the temporal and the spiritual realms. We can't possibly know all the dangers lying in wait for us as we go out into the world, so we pray that God will go with us and ahead of us.

The Collect for Peace also contains the lovely phrase "whose service is perfect freedom." We will shortly be leaving our service of worship to engage in serving God in the world. Yet our spiritual obedience to him is, paradoxically, perfect freedom. So, in the end, we do not need to fear anxiety, exhaustion, or despair.

Even after more than 450 years, these prayers are still vital and relevant in a world in which terrorism, nuclear weapons, and war are ongoing threats.

Votes and Prayers: Prayers for the State

We also say prayers for the State and the Church *(12–13* and *48–51)* and prayers of petition for the Queen and for all who are set in authority under her.

Some people have no time for politics or feel the church is no place to be praying for politicians. Yet when we pray for those who are in authority over us (even if we didn't vote for them), we are really praying for ourselves. The better they fulfil their duties, the better our world will be. These leaders need God's wisdom and grace so that "all things may be so ordered and settled by their endeavours upon the best and surest foundations, that peace and happiness, truth and justice, religion and piety may be established among us for all generations." So, for our own sake, we pray for those who are in authority over us, whether they accept our advice or not. We still don't have to vote for them.

Sermons and Prayers: Prayer for the Clergy and People (13)

The only time many of us give much thought to ministers is after their sermons, as we busily grade their efforts. If we spent as much time praying for them (perhaps while they prepare their sermons) as criticizing them, we might be quite astounded by the outcome, not only in their preaching but also in their pastoral ministry, which often goes unnoticed until we need it.

It is in our own best interest to pray for our clergy. We ask God "from whom cometh every good and perfect gift" to "send down upon our bishops and clergy, and all congregations committed to their charge, the healthful Spirit of thy grace; and that they may truly please thee, pour upon them the continual dew of thy blessing."

This prayer, like so many in the Prayer Book, works well, but not because the language is high-flown. It isn't. It's very direct. Nor are the ideas convoluted. Instead the prayer draws upon a memorable image. Yes, God's people get dry and exhausted and desperately need "the continual dew of thy blessing."

Laying Our Burdens before God: A Prayer for all Conditions of Men (14)

This prayer, written by Bishop Peter Gunning in 1661, is often included at this point because it embraces many concerns. In it, first of all we pray for *the whole world* and all the people it contains, that they may know God and the salvation or "saving health" he offers in Christ. This is the mission section where we pray for all peoples, cultures, and nations.

Secondly, we pray for *the whole Church* around the world, that it may be guided and ruled by the Holy Spirit, living in truth, upholding the faith, unified and at peace, living righteously. Such a tall order requires much prayer! The Church is a community of sinners forgiven, but until we reach heaven, still sinners. So the Church always needs to be infused with the power of the Holy Spirit and much prayer.

Thirdly, we pray for *all who are hurting*, whether mentally or physically, or who are in distressing circumstances.

beseech:	beg, plead
Catholic Church:	universal Church around the world
profess:	declare
commend:	entrust, commit
estate:	condition, circumstances
issue:	outcome, result

The Prayer for all Conditions of Men *(14)* at a Glance

The God Called Upon Or Invoked (The Invocation)

Creator	Our "Maker," as we say in the Apostles' and Nicene Creeds.
and Preserver	He continues to uphold us. We would die if he didn't.
of all mankind	He is the creator and preserver of all human beings, not just those who acknowledge him.
a compassionate Father (in final petition)	"we commend to thy fatherly goodness"

(cont'd on page 201)

The Prayer for all Conditions of Men at a Glance *(cont'd)*

For Whom	What Is Requested
1. All people from all walks of life All nations	make thy ways known unto them thy saving health (show them your salvation, save them: a plea for their salvation)
2. The Catholic Church, (that is) "the blessed company of all faithful people"	that it might be guided and governed by thy good [Holy] Spirit may be led in the way of truth may hold the faith in unity of spirit in the bond of peace in righteousness of life
3. All those afflicted or distressed in mind, body or estate [circumstances] (both Christian believers and others)	we commend (entrust) them to thy fatherly goodness comfort and relieve them give them patience under their sufferings and a happy issue out of all their afflictions

And this we beg for Jesus Christ his sake, *Amen.*

This prayer covers a lot of territory. Certainly, elsewhere in the book you can find prayers just for missions *(40–42)* or just for the Church *(42–48)* or just for those in sickness or anxiety *(54–55)*. But this prayer ensures, by placing them all under one roof, that we don't miss any of these crucial areas. This particular prayer is optional; others could be chosen. There is an excellent selection on *pages 37–58*, as we have seen. When we gather corporately or even in our private devotions, we must always remember to pray for others. Intercession itself is not optional.

Praying for the Forgotten: A General Intercession (57)

Another well-loved intercessory prayer that gathers up numerous concerns is A General Intercession *(57)*. Here we beg God "to remember for good" not only those who love us but even "those that hate us." We are praying for our enemies, as Jesus taught us to (Matthew 5:44). It also asks, "those whom we have forgotten, do thou, O Lord, remember." It recognizes our very human nature as well as God's astounding, all-encompassing love.

This prayer comes from an Eastern source, the ancient Greek Orthodox liturgy of St. Basil, and does not have the characteristically Western collect structure. Usually, Western collects open with a call or invocation to God that describes some aspect of his nature and then goes on to make certain requests that match those character traits. This supplication simply begins, "O Lord."

Only later, two-thirds of the way into the prayer, do we start to flesh out the picture of this God of ours. But it builds as a powerful creed of sorts, as we declare, "For thou art the Helper of the helpless, the Saviour of the lost, the Refuge of the wanderer, the Healer of the sick." We can confidently ask much of such a wonderful God.

A General Intercession *(57)*

O Lord,

Be mindful,	of those bowed before thee and of those absent through age, sickness or infirmity
care	for the infants
guide	the young
support	the aged
encourage	the faint-hearted
collect	the scattered [the spiritually lost]
bring	the wandering to thy fold
travel with	the voyagers

(cont'd on page 204)

A General Intercession *(cont'd)*

defend	the widows
shield	the orphans
deliver	the captives
heal	the sick
succour (help)	all who are in tribulation, necessity or distress
remember for good	all those that love us and those that hate us and those who have desired us to pray for them those we have forgotten

[Who is our God?]

Thou art: the Helper of the helpless
the Saviour of the lost
the Refuge of the wanderer
the Healer of the sick

Thou who knowest each man's need,
and hast heard his prayer
grant unto each according to thy merciful loving kindness
and thy eternal love
through Jesus Christ our Lord. *Amen.*

At the end, we actually pray the principles of supplication: God knows all our individual needs, he hears each of our prayers, and he will grant our requests in accord with his merciful love and kindness. His answers will not all make sense to us in this life, but in his "eternal love," they will.

A Really Big Thank–You: A General Thanksgiving (14)

Many Anglicans have memorized A General Thanksgiving *(14)* because it says so much, so well. Although it is one of the best loved prayers in the Book of Common Prayer, it was composed not by Archbishop Cranmer, but by Bishop Edward Reynolds (1599–1676). Sometimes the whole congregation is invited to pray it aloud with the priest. Watch how it actually shifts from thanksgiving to petition:

A General Thanksgiving *(14)*

Who is called upon?	Almighty God, Father of all mercies
Who is praying?	we thine unworthy servants
What type of prayer?	We ... give thee humble and hearty thanks
For what are we *thanking* this Father of all mercies?	for all thy goodness and loving kindness to us and to all men [particularly for ...]

(cont'd on page 206)

A General Thanksgiving (cont'd)

We bless [praise and
  thank] thee
                    for our creation
                      preservation
                      and all the blessings of this life
          but above all for thine inestimable love
                      in the redemption of the world by our
                      Lord Jesus Christ
                      [inestimable = unmeasurable]
          for the means of grace and for the
                      hope of glory

What do we ask for?
          We beseech [beg] thee
                      give us that due sense of all thy
                      mercies that our hearts may be
                      unfeignedly [sincerely] thankful
          And that we show forth thy praise
                      not only with our lips but in our lives
                      by giving up ourselves to thy service
                      and by walking before thee in
                      holiness and righteousness all
                      our days

Through whom do we pray
  & to whom do we
  give glory?
          Through Jesus Christ our Lord
          To whom with thee [the Father]
                      and the Holy Ghost, be all honour
                      and glory, world without end, *Amen.*

See how the prayer moves sequentially through time. We thank God first for our creation, then for our preservation, and next for all the blessings of this life. That's a lot! It speaks of our material or physical world.

Then it lists our spiritual blessings, again in a sequential order: We thank God for his love which is beyond measure, a love shown in the redemption of the world by our Lord Jesus Christ, for the means of grace and the hope of glory.

The next sentence captures the attitude of thanksgiving that only God can give: "Give us that due sense of all thy mercies that our hearts may be unfeignedly [genuinely] thankful."

Lip Service and Life Service

We will be leaving formal worship soon; so the final section of the General Thanksgiving reminds us that we are to show forth our praise to God "not only with our lips" in worship but also "in our lives, by giving up ourselves to thy service, and by walking before thee in holiness and righteousness all our days." We are to give God not only lip service but also life service. Such life service is sacrificial (we give up "ourselves") yet it is also amazingly liberating, as we acknowledged earlier in the Collect for Peace, "whose service is perfect freedom" *(11)*.

Warning to the Workaholic

Some may be tempted only to serve God out in the world, to be so busy with soup kitchens and healing ministries that they forget to take time to rest awhile with God. No one could have toiled more in service than Jesus, yet he took time to pray to his Father and to rest in his presence. We cannot spend all our time either worshipping in the sanctuary or serving in the soup kitchen. Both are necessary soul work.

Fulfil Now, O Lord: A Prayer of Saint Chrysostom (15)

The service draws to a close with a prayer that speaks of "our common supplications" and asks, "Fulfil now, O Lord, the desires and petitions of thy servants as may be most expedient [suitable] for them; granting us in this world knowledge of thy truth and in the world to come, life everlasting." What a context in which to place all our petitions! St. John Chrysostom (*c.*347–407) was an archbishop (or patriarch) of Constantinople, and was called *chryso-stomos* (golden-mouthed) for his eloquence.

In private prayer, some Anglicans occasionally substitute one of the lovely collects at the end of the Communion *(87–88)*.

God Has the Last Word: The Grace (15)

The closing prayer requests God's blessing over us. We are heading out into the week and into the world. There we will be greeted by curses and blasphemies as we live and work in a world that does not rightfully and fully acknowledge a holy God. We will be tempted to curse as well. So we desperately need God's blessing upon us, his benediction, which is the exact opposite of a curse.

Usually the prayer that is used is The Grace *(15)* of 2 Corinthians 13:14, which is Trinitarian. We ask that, "The grace of our Lord Jesus Christ and the love of God [the Father] and the fellowship of the Holy Ghost [Spirit] be with us all evermore." Grace, love, and community—what wonderful gifts!

Occasionally, a final burst of praise from the Acts of Praise *(62)* could be used. All proclaim God's glory. Three of the four scriptural sentences also speak of what God is able to do for us or has done for us as well. In your private devotions you might want to choose from this powerful selection to end your quiet time. Here is one:

> Now unto him who is able to do exceeding abundantly above all that we ask or think, according to the power that worketh in us, unto him be glory in the Church and in Christ Jesus, throughout all ages, world without end. *Amen.*
>
> (EPHESIANS 3:20–21)

Don't Bolt out the Door

We should take a few moments to pray silently before we leave. Simply to rush off from church now without greeting anyone would almost put the lie to "the fellowship of the Holy Ghost." Many churches offer tea, coffee, and fellowship after the service.

This is a good time to ask others what they would like prayer for or to hear how God has been working in their lives.

I Don't Get It??!!

While there generally isn't time in the service to ask a direct question, the people of God should be open to questions afterwards. Many churches now have websites or e-mail addresses so you can e-mail your questions. Most churches have libraries from which you can borrow books or tapes. You could take a course like Alpha or another study series. Being part of a small Bible-study or youth group helps. Or you might ask your priest for a mentor, someone you can question on an ongoing basis. An engaged couple is often paired with an older couple, while parents with a baby about to be baptized might be mentored by a couple with a young child. We're all in this together. And your questions help everyone think things through. The problem is not with people who ask questions but with people who don't.

Not Your Crowd?

Don't feel dismayed if, at first glance, the congregation doesn't look like the crowd you usually hang out with. If you want to hang out with God, then hang in; after the service, introduce yourself to the person in the pew beside you and to the minister or greeter at the door. Check out the coffee hour after the service and give it a few weeks. Pray that God will introduce you to someone you can feel comfortable with. These are people who may not look or sound like you, but as the people of God they are just like you, forgiven sinners wanting to encounter God. They are in the process of becoming holy, but just like you, they are not there yet.

What About Evensong? Mattins?

Evensong is another name for **Evening Prayer**, just as **Mattins** is another name for **Morning Prayer**. Some Anglican churches prefer to use these older names because they are reminders of the connection between our Daily Offices and the ones used by the pre-Reformation Church in England. (Note that calling the evening service Evensong does not necessarily mean that it is sung!)

Evening Prayer *(17)*

Now that you are familiar with **Morning Prayer,** you will quickly see that **Evening Prayer** *(17)* has the same basic structure. What makes **Evening Prayer** special is its beloved canticles and collects.

Evening Prayer allows us to make the Song of Mary and the Song of Simeon our own. They are often called by their Latin names, the *Magnificat* and the *Nunc Dimittis,* and both can be found in the opening chapters of Luke's Gospel, Mary's song in Chapter 1 and Simeon's in Chapter 2. Luke gets off to a singing start in these two chapters, which also include Zachariah's song, the *Benedicite,* and the angels' song to the shepherds.

No Exaggeration: The Magnificat (21)

Magnificat means "glorifies" in Latin: "My soul doth magnify [glorifies] the Lord." "Magnify" does not mean that Mary is exaggerating how magnificent God is, but rather that, as she praises God, she is stretching her own understanding of him. Adoration stretches our comprehension of how great and holy and powerful God is. You can supply the attribute: how eternal, how infinite, how loving, how pure, how trustworthy. When our view of God shrinks, we are the poorer.

The Church has made Mary's song its own. Early on, it was the canticle for Vespers in the Western Church, while in the Eastern Church it forms part of the Morning Office.

Turning the World Upside Down

Some people criticize the Church, claiming that it only supports the status quo, the people in power. But the *Magnificat* celebrates the way in which God creates big shake-ups. Look at all the reversals that happen when God shows the strength of his arm: "He hath scattered the proud in the imagination of their hearts," "He hath put down the mighty from their seat [of power], and hath exalted the humble and meek; He hath filled the hungry with good things and the rich he hath sent empty away." Today, there are many more Christians in the developing world, among the poor and the oppressed, than among the affluent of Europe and North America. The *Magnificat* is very much the prayer of the poor, trusting in God.

holpen:	helped

Mary's exuberant song of praise and thanksgiving echoes Hannah's song in the Old Testament (1 Samuel 2:1–10). To discover why Mary is rejoicing, start at Luke 1:26 and read to the end of the chapter.

Recognizing the Messiah: The Nunc Dimittis *(22)*

The *Nunc Dimittis*, the shortest of the canticles, is a lovely exit hymn, sung to a new arrival. The Holy Spirit had promised to Simeon, an aged and devout Jew, that he would not die until he had seen the Messiah. According to Jewish custom, firstborn male infants were brought to the temple in Jerusalem to be consecrated to the Lord. Simeon recognizes that this babe is the Saviour of both Jew and Gentile. He praises God while holding the newborn in his arms. Through Simeon's song, we, too, rejoice in our Messiah who redeems people from all nations.

Yet this lovely picture of an aged man cradling a tiny babe is bittersweet. Simeon also prophesies that "this child is destined to cause the falling and rising of many in Israel, and to be a sign that will be spoken against, so that the thoughts of many hearts will be revealed. And a sword will pierce your [Mary's] own soul too" (Luke 1:34-35). As this worldwide salvation is wrought, society will be turned upside down and both Mary and Jesus will suffer. So what seems a serene song of a grateful old man who can now die in peace also has a painful edge.

A Peace Which the World Cannot Give: Second Collect for Peace (23)

After praying the Collect of the Day, you will come to two collects that are a regular part of the service and well worth committing to memory. In the Second Collect for Peace *(23)*, we acknowledge that it is from God that "all holy desires, all good counsels and all just works do proceed." We recognize that as humans we cannot in our own power possess truly holy desires, give wise counsel, or do righteous acts. It is God who prompts all the desires, thoughts, and acts that please him. So, as God's servants we ask for:

1. that peace which the world cannot give;
2. that our hearts may be set to obey thy commandments;
3. that we being defended from the fear of our enemies may pass our time in rest and quietness.

A Prayer for the Paranoid—As Well As the Rest of Us: Third Collect, for Aid against All Perils (24)

Some of us are oblivious of the very real spiritual and physical dangers swirling around us. Others live in fear of anything and everything. This third collect, which also appears in **Compline,** is so brief and lovely that it can be memorized, even by the paranoid:

> Lighten our darkness, we beseech thee, O Lord; and by thy great mercy defend us from all perils and dangers of this night; for the love of thy only Son, our Saviour Jesus Christ. *Amen.*

Now more prayers and thanksgivings may be said, drawing from those found in **Morning Prayer** *(pages 12* to *14)* or elsewhere in the BCP (such as *pages 37* to *61*) but always ending with the Prayer of Saint Chrysostom on *page 24.*

Finally, **Evening Prayer,** like **Morning Prayer,** closes with the biblical Grace *(24)* found in 2 Corinthians 13:14. So in both Offices we hear God speaking to us through the Scriptures and we reply to him, often in the very words he has given us, by praying the psalms and canticles, and other biblically-shaped prayers.

Just do it!

When You Don't Feel Like Praying

Nothing is quite as satisfying or as frustrating as prayer. Like much that is worthwhile in life, it requires effort. Sometimes it is hard to get started. There is inertia. Be realistic about how much you should tackle. Then get on with it. The Puritans used to say, "Pray until you pray."

We speak of the discipline of prayer, and discipline suggests doing something difficult. We also talk of the habit of prayer. When a behaviour becomes a habit, it is actually easier to perform.

We habitually wash our faces and brush our teeth in the morning. We don't stare into the mirror and think, "Hey, should I wash my face today? How about my teeth? Do they need a brush this morning?" We don't wait to feel inspired before we wash up; we just get on and do it. And no matter how groggy we feel at the time, we always feel better afterwards.

Inspiration after Perspiration

Don't wait until you feel inspired to pray. Professional writers and artists don't wait to be inspired before they write or paint. They write or paint at least a little every day. Likewise, make prayer a habit. If we waited for inspiration, little would ever be written or painted or prayed in this world. Inspiration usually comes in the midst of much perspiration. We should pray simply because Jesus commanded us to pray. Often the feelings of inspiration follow upon our obedience to him. Prayer is a discipline that generally grows easier with time, although there will be some hard stretches too. (See page 224)

If you still don't feel like talking to God, if prayer doesn't seem real, tell him. Tell God whatever you're feeling.

Don't Overdo It!

Musicians and dancers accomplish more by practising a modest amount each day than by jamming everything into one huge rehearsal just before their performance. Athletes would collapse if they tried to pack all their training into one enormous session before the big game. It is not the total number of hours spent during the week that matters for musician or dancer or athlete so much as the daily regularity that will build up any skill. So whether you are trying to master a foreign language or the language of prayer, which can seem foreign at times, aim for a little often.

It is better to pray and read your Bible a little every day than to pray and read voraciously one day and then go prayerless for a week or more. Start with a few prayers each day, short Bible readings and a short psalm portion, whatever you can sustain. You are going to be praying over a lifetime, so build your spiritual muscles up gradually. What can you do in your life situation at this moment?

Setting unrealistic goals becomes self-defeating. Only increase your time when you have proven you can sustain a small amount. Be faithful in a little before you tackle more. You can set higher goals, but do so after the habit of prayer and Bible-reading is well established and you are really ready for more challenge.

A Rule of Life (555)

Many rules of prayer have developed in the history of the Church, but there has never been a uniform one. Rules of prayer are not meant to be strait-jackets limiting our communion with God. They teach the importance of regularity in our prayer life. The BCP suggests:

> Every Christian man or woman should from time to
> time frame a Rule of Life which may include:
> The regularity of attendance at public worship and
> especially at the Holy Communion.
> The practice of private prayer, Bible-reading and
> self-discipline ...
>
> *[excerpted from page 555]*

How long do we spend watching TV? Could we offer God fifteen or twenty minutes in the morning or evening, or both? Generally earlier is better, while we are still sharp and before the day fills up. God deserves "quality" time. Jesus got up early to pray (Mark 1:35). For some people, however, the morning is full of anxieties and distractions, and to "Be still and know that I am God" is more realistic in the evening. Choosing a time that will ensure regular devotions is the key.

Adapting the Daily Offices for Personal Devotions

Anglican priests and deacons are called upon to pray the Offices of **Morning** and **Evening Prayer** every day, either privately or in church *(lvi)*. As we have seen, these services are intended for lay people as well, so your participation is welcomed, either in church, or in the privacy of your own home.

You may wonder how you would ever find time to pray Morning Prayer every day. After all, as a sung church service, it is 60 to 90 minutes long. But at home there would be no announcements or hymns, no children's message, anthem, offering, or sermon. Nor would there be baptisms or special presentations or testimonies. And pieces that are sung or chanted in church can be said more quickly at home. You are now looking at about 15 to 20 minutes. This is still more demanding than the 5 to 10 minutes required for **Family Prayers** *(728)*.

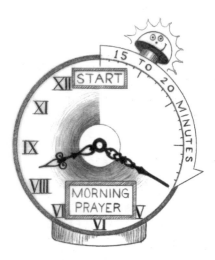

When you first begin incorporating **Morning** or **Evening Prayer** into your personal devotions or when time presses, try shortening the services by including only the most essential elements.

Here is what you should include in **Morning Prayer,** for example, with some suggestions as to how to work up gradually to the full service.

One scriptural sentence (after which you might jump down to the confession.)

The Exhortation: In private prayer only the first paragraph needs to be used.

Confession: If you say *both* **Morning** and **Evening Prayer,** you might choose to say the confession only in the evening and can begin **Morning Prayer** on *page 6* with "O Lord, open thou our lips" (see page *lvi,* General Rubrics, paragraph 20). The confession is always said, however, on the penitential mornings of Ash Wednesday and Good Friday.

Instead of the Absolution that only a priest can pronounce, pray *one* of the following prayers for pardon:

"O God, whose nature and property ..." *(58)*
Collect for 21st Sunday after Trinity *(252)* (briefest)
Collect for 24rd Sunday after Trinity *(257)*
"For Pardon through the Cross" *(730)*

A Canticle: The shortest canticle is the *Jubilate Deo* (Psalm 100 on *page 457*). This burst of joy is only four verses long, so it is ideal for the absolute beginner or for days when there really is precious little time.

Next, get comfortable with the classic three canticles found within **Morning Prayer** before venturing on to pray the other three found in the Additional Canticles section *(25)*. Repeat the first three twice over six days:

Monday and Thursday: *Venite (6)*
Tuesday and Friday: *Te Deum (7)*
Wednesday and Saturday: *Benedictus (9)*

When you are more familiar with the Prayer Book and are ready for more variety, you can pray one canticle each day:

Monday   *Venite (6)* "O come, let us sing unto the Lord" (Psalm 95)
You can end with "the sheep of his hand."

Tuesday   *Te Deum (7)* "We praise thee, O God"
The third section can be dropped if time presses.

Wednesday *Benedictus (9)* "Blessed be the Lord God of Israel" (St. Luke 1:68)
Zechariah's song

or *Jubilate Deo (457)* "O be joyful in the Lord" (Psalm 100) which is brief but beautiful.

Thursday *Benedicite (26)* "O, All ye works of the Lord, Bless ye the Lord"
The Song of the Three Children
To shorten it, you can say the refrain only at the end of each section.

Friday *Cantate Domino (28)* "Sing unto the Lord a new song" (Isaiah 42:10)

Saturday *Surge, Illumine (28)* "Arise, shine, for thy light has come" (Isaiah 60:1)
A favourite song during Advent and Epiphany.

If you have said the *Te Deum* with its wonderful Trinitarian credo in your private devotions, you could skip the Apostles' Creed if time presses. Feel free to add your own prayers of intercession and thanksgiving, either from the rich variety in the Prayer Book or from your own spontaneous thoughts. The most important thing to note is that if you do decide to take up the discipline of the Daily Offices, you should aim to stick with the appointed psalms (either the one-month or the two-month cycle) and the Bible readings from the daily lectionary. They are really the core and backbone of **Morning** and **Evening Prayer.**

Making Your Mark: Flags and Bookmarks

If you own your own Book of Common Prayer, you can slip or glue-gun a five-ribbon bookmark into your copy. These can be purchased at most bookstores. Then the appointed collects and psalms will be close at hand. Or you may prefer the colourful little flags that can be removed and rearranged several times before they lose their adhesion. Not everyone is happy with these markers. Some people find they damage the page.

Small index cards are a safe bet. Insert an index card beside A Prayer for all Conditions of men *(14)*. You can then list those you are praying for who are "afflicted in mind, body or estate." On the reverse side, list those gifts for which you are particularly grateful and mention them when you say the General Thanksgiving *(14)*. While there isn't much space on an index card for details, such lists will help you recall key people and events. Date the card and write a new one at least each month. If you want to record more information, you could keep a prayer journal.

Spiritual Dryness

There are seasons when even the most devoted Christian finds his or her conversation with God has dried up, when the relationship seems distant. It is as if a loved one has gone away on a journey for a while. You still have to keep sending letters and leaving messages until she returns. And she will return. She is faithful. In fact, when she returns, there will be even more to talk about, more to share, more intimacy after the absence. Best of all, you will no longer take her for granted.

Of course, God is always present. He only seems absent from our minds or hidden from our senses. We need to show our trust in him by hanging in when he seems hidden, by remaining faithful.

Here are some points to consider during a dry stretch:

▶ Could some unconfessed sin be blocking my relationship with God?

▶ Am I taking God for granted? Is my view of God too small?

▶ Read a new devotional book, or reread a classic that will awaken your appreciation for God.

(cont'd on page 226)

Points to Consider (cont'd)

▶ Read biographies of famous Christians and note their down times as well as their victories. You are not alone.

▶ Pray Psalm 22. The psalmist also felt abandoned by God. Tell God how you feel.

▶ Listen to some new Christian music.

▶ Don't stop praying but try some new approaches. Try a new space or time for prayer. Could you pray outside in nature or even while commuting? Try a prayer walk or jog.

▶ Try some new ways of praying. Say different canticles. Try the *Magnificat* in the morning or the **Litany** instead of **Morning Prayer.** Go for a shorter stretch, perhaps with the briefer **Family Prayers,** but don't eliminate prayer entirely.

▶ Attend a different service than usual or visit a different church to gain a fresh perspective.

▶ Attend a Christian course, conference, or retreat.

▶ If you have a working knowledge of a foreign language, try reading your Bible in that language, whether French or Spanish or Mandarin, perhaps with a dual-language translation. The Canadian Bible Society carries a wide selection of parallel texts (1-800-465-2425). You will gain a fresh perspective on familiar phrases and will not be as likely to rush over the text, but will actually sink into it and study it and draw more from it.

▶ Don't try to force the same level of intensity in a relationship day in, day out. Things fluctuate. You may have had an ecstatic mountaintop experience once, but

(cont'd on page 227)

Points to Consider (cont'd)

you cannot live your whole life on the mountaintop. God is going to meet you in new ways and in unexpected places. You can find him even on the plains and in the valleys. Christ, too, spent time in the desert. Keep journeying with him wherever he leads.

▶ In times of extreme stress or grief, ask for and depend upon the prayers of others. Be upheld by their prayers. Remember that groans and tears are prayers, too. Offer even your sorrows to God. Don't expect a lot of yourself.

▶ If you are bored, you may be under-challenged. When we are pushed to our limits and struggling on life's learning curves, we cling more closely to God. Is God calling you to serve him in a new way out in the world, where you will be stretched?

▶ Talk to a spiritual mentor. Priests are called not just to preach in church publicly but to pastor privately. Seek your minister's spiritual counsel.

▶ Ask another Christian you trust and respect to pray for you during this dry stretch.

▶ Check your medical condition. Our physical health affects our spiritual health. Low haemoglobin, depression and insomnia all need medical attention. Pray that God will heal your whole person: mind, body and spirit.

▶ Our God is a God of surprises. Be expectant. Know it will pass. God is faithful.

Like a close friendship or marriage, our encounters with God sometimes need to be revitalized.

Ever Ancient and Ever New

St Augustine (354–430), an adult convert to Christianity, exclaimed, "Too late came I to love thee, O thou Beauty both so ancient and so fresh."[25] He regretted that he had not loved God all his life. But he also captures the ancient yet ever-fresh paradox of our living God.

Some people reject the Book of Common Prayer as too old. Yet that is its very strength. As twenty-first century Christians, we are part of a praying community, a prayer continuum that stretches back not just 450 years, to Thomas Cranmer, but, as we have seen, even further back to the early church and the people of God in the Old Testament. In the Book of Common Prayer, we pray the 1600-year-old *Te Deum*, we affirm the 1700-year-old creeds, we pray the two-millennia-old Lord's Prayer, *Magnificat, Benedictus,* and *Nunc Dimittis,* and we sing 3,000-year-old psalms. And we also rejoice with the eternal, ever-new songs of heaven, the songs of the angels and the heavenly host that are echoed in the *Sanctus*, "Holy, Holy Holy"; the *Agnus Dei* "O Lamb of God"; and the *Gloria in Excelsis* "Glory be to God on high" in **Holy Communion** *(79, 84, 86)* and in the anthem for Good Friday *(173)*, "Worthy is the Lamb." So we pray ancient and eternal, ever-young prayers that will renew and refresh our conversations and encounters with our living and everlasting God who is himself "Beauty both so ancient and so fresh."

Learn to Pray by Praying

The temptation is to read a lot about prayer but never actually to pray. If you want to dance the salsa, at some point you have to kick up your heels on the dance floor. If you want to learn to swim, you have to get wet. If you want to parachute, you have to jump out of the plane and pull the rip cord. Charts, manuals, and instructor-led demonstrations can only take you so far. You won't really get it until you actually do it.

There are plenty of books to read on prayer; but before you pick up another, put this one down and ask God to help you start praying. Even that request is a petition, so you will already have begun! Ask him to help you pray not only across the day, but also across your lifetime. After all, God longs to converse intimately with you, now and forever.

Recipes can be fascinating reading, but they are no substitute for the delicious dish itself. Here are some recipes for prayer. May they encourage you to pray, but remember, take time to feast at the real banquet.

Pondering Prayer[26]

When you pray, know before whom you stand.

The Talmud

We beseech God with his own word.

St. Cyprian

The value of persistent prayer is not that he will hear us ... but that we will finally hear him.

William McGill

We call prayer ... that speech of man to God which, whatever else is asked, ultimately asks for the manifestation of the divine Presence.

Martin Buber

Prayer is an invitation to God to intervene in our lives.

Abraham Joshua Herschel

When we pray, we immerse ourselves in the living presence of God.

E. H. Peterson

Prayer is homesickness for God. Habitual prayer is a condition of life in continual conversation, continual reference to God.

Robert Crouse

(cont'd on page 231)

Pondering Prayer (cont'd)

Prayer nurtures our need for
intimacy with God. Prayer invigorates
the heart and sustains the friendship
we have with a personal God.

J.I. Packer

Worship is for God. Worship is eternal,
and is something God sweeps us into
—in fact the thing he made us for
in the first place.

Anthony Burton

You need not cry very loud. He is
nearer to us than we think.

Brother Lawrence

Prayer enlarges the heart until it is
capable of containing God's gift of
himself.

Mother Teresa

Thou hast made us for thyself,
O Lord, and our hearts are restless
until they find their rest in thee.

St. Augustine

Seek His Face

Christians do not pray to an unknown god or to an unknowable
god. We pray to a God who reveals himself as our loving Father,
who reveals himself by the power of his Holy Spirit in the face of
Jesus.

Seek ye my face! ...
Thy face, Lord, will I seek.

(PSALM 27:8, KJV)

Before they call, I will answer.
While they are still speaking, I will hear.

(ISAIAH 65:24)

The Lord is near to all who call on him,
To all who call on him in truth.

(PSALM 145:18)

Draw near to God and he will draw near to you.

(JAMES 4:8, RSV)

Appendix: Where did the BCP come from?

This appendix provides a bit of historical background to the Book of Common Prayer, focussing on the turbulent times in which it originated and the religious issues that shaped its development. (If you find beheadings, imprisonment, burning at the stake, and book-burnings dull, skip this appendix.)

A Vulgar Tongue

The Book of Common Prayer first came into being in the middle of the sixteenth century, at the height of the Reformation in Europe. This was a time of great controversy, with much religious and political turmoil between Protestants and Roman Catholics. People described the Prayer Book as written in "the vulgar tongue," in other words, in English. Some people would have meant this as a compliment, others as an insult! Today, when we say that someone's language is "vulgar," we mean that it is rude, obscene, or indecent. However, in the fifteenth and sixteenth centuries, people who wanted to reform the Church were consciously attempting to produce a "vulgar" Bible and a "vulgar" prayer book!

?

Vulgar is Middle English and comes from the Latin *vulgaris,* meaning "of the common people." So the older meaning of *vulgar* is "popular", or "in common use." A "vulgar" tongue means a language spoken by the common people. In England, until late in the Middle Ages, the royal court spoke French while church services were conducted in Latin. In fact, all over Western Europe after the fall of the Roman Empire, Latin was the language of learning and literacy. By the late Middle Ages, there was a great divide between those who could understand Latin and those who could not. The English peasant or shopkeeper could not understand court French or church Latin—only English.

One of the principles of the sixteenth-century reformers was that the Scriptures should be available to all people in their own language, and that public worship should also be conducted in a known, not an unknown, tongue. In contrast at that time, the Church of Rome, fearing that uneducated folk would misinterpret Scripture or question church teachings, insisted that only priests should read and interpret the Latin Bible. So at the very start of the Reformation in England, one of the first tasks that the reformers set themselves was to translate the Bible into English. This had to be done in secret, because it was illegal for people to own or read a Bible in English, and anyone breaking this law could be imprisoned or put to death.

A Royal Eye-Opener

In 1536, one of these courageous translators, William Tyndale, was arrested and sentenced to be executed. As he went to his death, he called out in a loud voice, "Lord, open the King of England's eyes!" God answered Tyndale's dying prayer. In 1539, English reformers, including Thomas Cranmer, the Archbishop of Canterbury, actually convinced King Henry VIII to have an English translation of the Bible placed in every parish church.

Admittedly, one major reason why Henry supported the start of the Reformation in England was that he wanted to divorce his wife, Catherine of Aragon. Catherine had not produced a male heir, and Anne Boleyn, a lady at the royal court, had caught his eye. Henry was anxious to have a son to succeed him because England had passed through a bloody civil war not many years earlier, and he feared that a daughter would too easily come under the influence of warring factions. His conscience also troubled him because Catherine was the widow of his dead brother, and he had become convinced that marrying his brother's wife was a sin.

In the Roman Catholic Church, divorce was allowed in special circumstances, if a decree of annulment was obtained from the Pope. However, the Pope refused to grant this decree. Catherine's powerful uncle, the king of Spain, was at that very moment besieging Rome with his army, and the Pope did not dare invite more trouble.

Henry had wide support among the English bishops, because for centuries the popes had been claiming more and more authority over the once-independent English Church. So, with the bishops' support, Henry broke with Rome and declared himself the head of the Church in England.

Yet Henry was in many respects still Catholic. He believed in transubstantiation (the conversion, after consecration, of the bread and wine into the physical Body and Blood of Christ), and withholding the Communion cup from lay people. He also supported priestly celibacy and binding monastic vows (despite the fact that he destroyed the monasteries to finance his wars abroad!) The old Catholic, Latin church services remained intact until Henry's death. It would take several more years and a prayer book in English to reform the Church beyond translating the Bible into English.

A Vulgar Prayer Book

The first Book of Common Prayer came into use in England in 1549, shortly after the death of Henry VIII. It was introduced during the short reign of his young son, Edward VI (1547–1553), who came to the throne when he was only nine years of age. Thomas Cranmer, still the Archbishop of Canterbury, was its chief architect. In compiling the Book of Common Prayer, Cranmer went back to the ancient Latin liturgy of the Catholic Church in England, revising it and adapting it to reflect

Protestant lines of thought. The Prayer Book was slightly modified in 1552, but young Edward died shortly afterwards at only 15 years of age, and his older stepsister, Mary Tudor came to the throne.

Mary was a devout Roman Catholic. During her reign (1553–1558), the Prayer Book was banned and Cranmer, its great compiler, was imprisoned. Cranmer, along with many others, was burned at the stake for refusing to convert back to Roman Catholicism. It seemed as though the Prayer Book would not survive either.

In 1558, Mary died childless and her half-sister, Elizabeth I ascended the throne (1558–1603). Elizabeth was a firm supporter of the Reformation; "A Prayer for the Queen and all in Authority" *(13)* was actually adapted from a prayer that she herself wrote. The Book of Common Prayer was restored the next year with a few small changes, and was used continuously for the next 86 years.

Did Shakespeare Pray from the Book of Common Prayer?

William Shakespeare (1564–1616) would have been familiar with the Book of Common Prayer. The first edition came out in 1549, fifteen years before he was born.

At the start of the sixteenth century, there was an almost volcanic explosion in the English language. The French and Italians experienced a renaissance in art and sculpture while the English experienced a great flowering in language arts. The works of Shakespeare are part of the rich fruit of this age. The BCP, however, is much more easily understood than Shakespeare. Although its beauty is similar, the BCP was deliberately written in a clear and accessible style that would speak to the hearts, minds, and souls of worshippers from every walk of life.

The Middle Way of Anglicanism

Through the turbulent Reformation, the Anglican Church walked what has been called a *via media* or "middle way." Like other moderate Protestants in Europe, the reformers of the English Church were concerned with correcting certain errors, abuses, and superstitions that had crept into the churches under Rome over the centuries, which they believed had obscured and distorted the whole truth of our salvation in Christ. Unlike the most radical Protestant reformers, such as the Anabaptists, they did not aim to discard their inherited tradition and start afresh. They were intent on pruning, not uprooting.

More than other moderate Protestants, the English reformers tried, in the Book of Common Prayer, to maintain the greatest possible continuity with the ancient catholic tradition of worship as they had received it. We can truly claim that the English Church that came through this process and the Book of Common Prayer, which is one of its fruits, are both catholic and

reformed. In time, this continuity with ancient catholic tradition
was recognized as making the worship of the reformed and
protestant Church of England unique.

The Anglican reformers drew up the Articles of Religion *(698)*
to define the Anglican position in response to the controversies
of the day. Finalized in 1571, they are often called the Thirty-
Nine Articles.

Some of these articles were written to show that the position of
the reformers was completely consistent with the ancient,
undivided Christian Church in such key doctrines as the Trinity,
the Incarnation, the death and resurrection of Christ, the full
divinity and the full humanity of Christ, and the divinity of the
Holy Spirit. Other articles addressed points on which the
Anglican reformers considered the Roman Church and the
radical Protestants to be mistaken.

Anglican Answers

*In response to some of the Roman teachings, the
Thirty-Nine Articles declared:*

1. We are justified by faith not works. "We are accounted
   righteous before God, only for the merit of our Lord and
   Saviour Jesus Christ by Faith, and not for our own works
   or deservings ..." *(Article 11)*
2. Christ is "the only Mediator between God and Man."
   (Article 7)

(cont'd on page 240)

Anglican Answers (cont'd)

3. The Pope is not infallible in spiritual matters. *(Article 19)* and "has no jurisdiction in this Realm of England." *(Article 37)*

4. The Church of Rome and General Councils have erred in the past and may err again in the future. *(Articles 19, 21)*

5. Public prayer and the ministry of the Sacraments must be in a language understood by the people, not in an unknown tongue such as Latin. *(Article 24)*

6. Clergy may marry. *(Article 32)*

7. The Communion cup is not to be denied to the lay people. *(Article 30)* [Rome allowed the laity to receive only the bread.]

8. Purgatory, paying for pardons, worshipping images, and praying to saints are all denounced. *(Article 22)*

9. The sufficiency of Scripture for salvation is maintained. *(Articles 6, 20)*

10. The Apocrypha (books which are only included in some ancient versions of the Bible and not in others) should not be used to establish any church teachings. Teachings are to be based only on the books of the Old and New Testaments which have been universally received by the Church. *(Article 6)*

11. The Roman doctrine of transubstantiation in Holy Communion is denied. The bread and wine do not become the actual flesh and blood of Christ. Instead, "The Body of Christ is given, taken and eaten, in the Supper, only after an heavenly and spiritual manner." And this is all received by "Faith." *(Article 28)*

12. There can be considerable variety in the traditions and ceremonies of various churches, as long as nothing is done against God's Word. *(Article 34)*

(cont'd on page 241)

Anglican Answers *(cont'd)*

In response to some of the teachings of the radical Protestants, the Thirty-Nine Articles declared:

1. There has never been any sinless person except Christ. All of us fall into sin even after we are baptized. However, by God's grace we are enabled to repent. *(Articles 15 and 16)* [Some Anabaptists believed that anyone who had been baptized was no longer capable of sin. Others believed that sin committed after baptism was unforgivable.]
2. Infant baptism is an acceptable practice for the children of believers. *(Article 27)* [Anabaptists believed only in adult "believer's baptism" and so rebaptized converts who had been baptized as infants.]
3. Ministers must be lawfully called and sent (ordained). They cannot be self-appointed. *(Article 23)* It is lawful to have archbishops and bishops. *(Article 36)* [Anabaptists opposed the church hierarchy of bishops, priests, and deacons.]
4. Even if an evil minister preaches and administers the sacraments, God can still use his Word and Sacraments to good effect if the one who receives them does so in faith. *(Article 26)*
5. Property does not have to be held in common. *(Article 38)* [Anabaptists taught a kind of Christian communism that did not allow for private property.]
6. Christians may swear a solemn oath in court. (*Article 39)* [Anabaptists would not take judicial oaths, and some would not hold public office.]
7. A Christian could bear arms to serve in a war. *(Article 37)* [Some Anabaptists were pacifists, and many separated from the world to set up their own Christian communities.]

Books for Bonfires

In 1645, Puritans gained control of Parliament, banned the Book of Common Prayer, and beheaded King Charles I. In those days the Book of Common Prayer was the favourite fuel for book-burnings. If you had been living in England between 1645 and 1662, and it was found in your possession, you could have been fined or imprisoned. The BCP was forbidden not only for congregational use but even for private devotions!

Those who wanted the Prayer Book destroyed during that period were Protestants who opposed "set" prayers. They even forbade the reciting of the Lord's Prayer! These prayer-book-burners loved the Bible, yet paradoxically the Prayer Book they despised was overflowing with Scripture.

Finally, in 1660, Charles II became king of England, and the Anglican Church was restored along with the Book of Common Prayer. The BCP was revised in 1662, and that version has remained the official book of worship of the Church of England to this day. It was at this time that the King James Version of the Bible, which had been completed in 1611, was first adopted for the BCP Epistles and Gospels. For the psalms, the powerful original translation done in 1535 by Miles Coverdale (1488–1568) was retained.

In 1689, the Act of Toleration kept the Anglican Church as England's state church or official religion (which it still is) but also guaranteed religious freedom for all Protestant dissenters. Roman Catholics were given religious freedom through a series of later laws in 1778, 1791, and 1829.

Your "Average" Anglican Today

In the eighteenth and nineteenth centuries, with the expansion of the British Empire and vigorous missionary work, Anglicanism and the Book of Common Prayer, in numerous translations, spread around the world. Today, your average Anglican is not British or even North American, and is certainly not white or middle-aged. On any given Sunday, there are now more Anglicans attending church in the West African state of Nigeria than in the United Kingdom, the United States, Canada, Australia, and New Zealand all combined!

Some of the most vibrant Anglican communities exist in sub-Saharan Africa, in Asia, and in Latin America. Anglicanism's centre of gravity has dramatically shifted south, from the developed to the developing world, from secure and prosperous places to areas facing the challenges of poverty, oppression, and persecution.

Canadian BCP—Eh?

While Anglicanism spread to every province and territory in Canada, Canada never established a state church. The Anglican Church of Canada revised the Book of Common Prayer in 1918, rewording some archaic language and adding some new prayers specifically for Canada such as: "For the Prime Minister and the Premiers of the Provinces" *(49)*, "For Parliament and the Legislature of the Province" *(50)* and also thanksgivings "For our National Heritage" and "For Confederation" *(59)* and two collects for Canada *(278* and *281).*

A further Canadian revision in 1962 removed from public worship some harsh verses in the psalms that are discussed in Chapter Four, page 167. It added the just-before-bed **Order for Compline** *(722)* that is described in Chapter Three, page 110. It also revised the **Service for Children**, and renamed it the **Service for Young People** *(622).* Here, even "our play" is offered to God, and we are reminded that God revealed himself to Samuel while the prophet was still a child. The opening prayer rings with a clarity that adults can appreciate too:

> Lord, teach us to pray. Lord, keep our thoughts from wandering. Lord, cleanse our hearts that we may worship thee in spirit and in truth; through Jesus Christ our Lord. *Amen.*
>
> *(622)*

Index of Collects and Other Prayers in the BCP

This subject index should help you unearth and locate (sometimes in odd spots) what you need in the Book of Common Prayer.

Being formed in Christ

Boldness in witness to Christ *(108, 278* [1st], *310, 320* [2nd])
Confidence in God's promises *(107)*
Constancy in faith *(117, 214, 262, 272, 274)*
Daily work *(319, 732* [1st])
Fasting and self-discipline *(95, 115* [2nd], *131, 140, 190)*
Forgiveness of enemies *(614* [3rd])
Fruits of the Spirit *(277, 618* [2nd])
Gift of God's grace *(104, 115* [1st], *119, 203, 205* [2nd], *217, 231, 234, 247, 249, 271, 305, 311)*
Guidance and right judgement *(123, 196, 205* [1st], *231, 249)*
Healing of infirmities *(286)*
Holy living *(182, 244, 259, 731* [4th])
Humility and obedience *(150, 237, 260, 288)*
Illumination *(110, 117, 289)*
Increase of faith, hope and charity *(136, 239)*
Innocence of life *(111, 190)*
Knowledge of Scripture *(87* [3rd], *97, 295)*
Membership in the communion of saints *(56, 275, 299, 301, 302, 304, 309, 316, 600* [3rd])
Nourishment in true faith *(205* [2nd], *228)*
Perseverance *(87* [4th], *635)*
Prayer *(221, 622* [1st])
Purity of heart *(67* [2nd], *201, 247, 266)*

Right asking *(233)*
Right receiving of Holy Communion *(169* [2nd], *83* [2nd])
Right use of this world's goods *(292, 618* [1st], *734* [2nd], *735)*
Seeking for God *(625* [1st])
Steadfast love of God *(194, 219, 226)*
Taking up the cross and following Christ *(260, 274, 321* [1st])
Thankfulness to God *(191, 283* [2nd])
To be buried and raised with Christ *(180, 184, 727* [2nd])

Praise

Canticles *(6, 7, 9, 21, 22, 25, 26, 28)*
Scripture *(62, 104, 173, 182, 204, 573* [2nd])
"Blessed art thou …" *(725)*
"Glory be to God on high …" *(86)*

Penitence

Confession *(4, 77, 84, 581, 613–614, 622, 726* [1st], *730* [2nd])
Appeals for God's mercy *(58* [2nd], *132, 138, 147, 223, 236,*
    257, 629 [1st])
Prayers for pardon *(147, 252, 257, 614* [2nd], *730* [3rd])
Words of comfort *(77–78)*

Trust and resignation

In the morning *(729* [2nd])
At night *(58* [1st], *723* [1st], *727* [5th])
In time of bad harvest *(619)*
For the sick *(321, 579–580)*
For the dying *(588–590)*
Not fearing death *(599* [2nd and 3rd])

At the death of a child *(606–607)*
At the burial of the dead *(599–600, 603, 608)*

Thanksgivings

Canada *(59)*
Commonwealth *(60)*
Deliverance from peril *(60, 636)*
Ending of civil or industrial strife *(61)*
Favourable weather *(60)*
General thanksgiving *(14, 307, 736)*
Gift of a child *(575* [1st])
God's blessings *(626* [2nd])
God's gifts displayed in his people *(317)*
God's Word *(264, 283* [2nd])
Harvest *(617–620)*
Medical science *(61)*
Missions *(58)*
Recovery from sickness *(61)*

Blessings and closing prayers

*(If the one saying a blessing is not a priest, it is usual to replace "you"
and "your" in those prayers by "us" and "our".)*

(15, 58 [2nd]*, 86* [2nd]*, 87, 88, 186* [2nd]*, 601* [3rd and 4th])

Petition and supplication

General

A general intercession *(57)*
Prayer for all conditions of men *(14)*
A bidding prayer *(62)*
Prayer and intercession *(729)*
Intercession *(75)*
Litany (30)

For the state and work of the Church

Defence of God's people *(148, 242)*
Extension of the Church *(40–41, 121, 320* [1st], *618* [3rd])
God's protection over the Church *(240, 254)*
Health of the Church universal *(39, 193)*
Ministry of all members of the Church *(174* [2nd], *317)*
Missionaries and mission societies *(42, 58, 314, 625* [3rd])
Salvation of all people *(16–17, 142)*
To be kept faithful in God's truth *(110, 129, 285, 291)*
To be preserved from false apostles *(268)*
Unity of all Christians *(40, 297)*

For individuals and groups in the Church

Bishops *(312, 657, 667* [1st], *670)*
Clergy *(46* [2nd], *655* [3rd], *670* [2nd], *671* [3rd])
Clergy and congregations *(13* [2nd], *283* [1st])
The parish *(43, 44, 736)*
Vacancy of a parish *(45)*
Diocese or deanery *(43)*

Synods *(42, 43)*
Conference or retreat *(323)*
Parochial mission *(326)*
Sunday schools *(47, 625* [2nd and 4th])
Confirmation candidates *(47, 48, 559, 560)*
Those about to be called to an office *(210)*
Those seeking ordination *(46, 646)*
Theological colleges and students (*45, 47)*
Church building *(679* [2nd], *689* [3rd], *691* [1st])

For family and friends

Birthday *(115* [3rd], *734)*
Child, children *(531* [1st and 2nd], *733)*
Family *(732)*
Gift of a child *(570* [3rd])
Loved ones absent or departing *(633, 733* [2nd and 3rd])
Married couple *(570–571)*
Parents and children *(625* [1st], *626* [1st])
Relatives and friends (Christian and non-Christian) *(732)*
Right observance of Sunday *(48)*
Travellers *(54, 633)*
Faithful departed *(600* [4th], *601* [1st], *603* [1st], *608* [3rd])

Spiritual defence and protection

Angelic help and defense *(294)*
Defence against all enemies *(11* [3rd], *145)*
Defence against perils at night *(723, 726–727)*
Defence of body and soul *(23* [4th], *87* [2nd], *143)*
For God's direction and protection *(124, 198, 219, 561* [1st],
    615 [1st])
From all adversity *(134, 221, 250)*

Exploring Words
Used in the BCP

by Diana Verseghy

A. How do those strange verbs work?

In Chapter 1, we looked briefly at examples of some forms of verbs (action words) in the BCP that you may not be familiar with. Let's examine these verb forms in more detail.

The archaic second person singular (thou)

As we saw, "thou" is used in the BCP when speaking to a single other person, instead of "you" which we now use when talking to either one or many other persons. (When addressing more than one person, the BCP uses "ye". For example, "Ye that do truly and earnestly repent …")

For actions occurring in the present, the verbs used with "thou" take the ending *-st* or *-est:*

you know	*thou knowest*
you keep	*thou keepest*
you forgive	*thou forgivest*
you take	*thou takest*
you save	*thou savest*
you receive	*thou receivest*
you lead	*thou leadest*
you hear	*thou hearest*
you say	*thou sayest*
you see	*thou seest*
you flee	*thou fleest*

you go	*thou goest*
you do	*thou doest*
you have	*thou hast*
you are	*thou art*

The last two verbs don't quite follow the overall pattern, but they are the only unusual ones. Note, in pronouncing these words, that the ending *-est* is always pronounced as a separate syllable: so for example "seest" is not pronounced the same way as "ceased", but as two syllables: "SEE-est" (likewise "SAVE-est", "FLEE-est", "GO-est", "DO-est").

For actions taking place in the past, the same endings *-st* or *-est* are simply added to the basic past form of the verb that we are familiar with today:

you knew	*thou knewest*
you kept	*thou keptest*
you forgave	*thou forgavest*
you took	*thou tookest*
you saved	*thou savedst*
you received	*thou receivedst*
you led	*thou leddest*
you heard	*thou heardest*
you said	*thou saidst*
you saw	*thou sawest*
you fled	*thou fleddest*
you went	*thou wentest*
you did	*thou didst*
you had	*thou hadst*
you were	*thou wert*

"Wert" doesn't quite follow the above rule, but again, it's the only one. Just as we saw with the ending *-est*, the ending *-edst* is always pronounced as a separate syllable: "SAVE-edst", "RECEIVE-edst".

For complex verb forms in the past, present or future, that is where we would normally use the verb with "have", "does" and "will", these words change to their "thou" forms of "hast", "doth" and "wilt":

you have spoken	*thou hast spoken*
you do send	*thou dost send*
you will go	*thou wilt go*

One more thing that you may be wondering about is when to use "thee". "Thou" is used when we speak of a person doing an action, as is the case in all of the examples above. "Thee" is used when we speak of a person to whom an action is being done. Here are some illustrations:

we praise you	*we praise thee*
I call upon you	*I call upon thee*
they turn to you	*they turn to thee*
we speak of you	*we speak of thee*
I am with you	*I am with thee*

If we are talking about more than one person to whom an action is being done, "you" is used. (As we saw at the beginning of this section, for more than one person doing an action, "ye" is used.)

And that's all you need to know about the use of "thou" and "thee"!

The third person singular (he, she, it)

For actions performed by a single person or thing in the present, the BCP uses the sixteenth-century ending *-th* or *-eth,* instead of the ending *-s* or *-es* that we are accustomed to today. For example:

the sun rises	*the sun riseth*
she finds	*she findeth*
the king reigns	*the king reigneth*
he leads	*he leadeth*

Jesus lives	*Jesus liveth*
the woman rejoices	*the woman rejoiceth*
the warrior slays	*the warrior slayeth*
he lets	*he letteth*
God sits	*God sitteth*
she has	*she hath*
Peter sees	*Peter seeth*
the arrow flies	*the arrow flieth*
she goes	*she goeth*
he does	*he doeth*
John says	*John saith*

Note in pronouncing these words that as in the case of *-est* above, the ending *-eth* is always pronounced as a separate syllable: so for example "seeth" is not pronounced the same way as "seethe", but as two syllables: "SEE-eth" (likewise "RISE-eth", "LIVE-eth", "GO-eth", "DO-eth". "Flieth" is pronounced "FLY-eth"). There is just one exception to this rule: "saith" is usually pronounced "SETH" rather than "SAY-eth".

For complex verb forms describing actions in the past or present, where we would normally use the verb in combination with "has" or "does", these words change to "hath" or "doth":

she has gone	*she hath gone*
God has spoken	*God hath spoken*
Mary does see	*Mary doth see*
he does take	*he doth take*

And that's all you need to know about verbs in the third person!

Other odd verb forms

A few verb forms found in the BCP for actions in the past are a little peculiar. Some verbs that today would have an *-o-* in the past tense have an *-a-* instead in the Elizabethan form:

God spoke	*God spake*
they broke	*they brake*
you bore	*thou barest* (singular), *ye bare* (plural)
we swore	*we sware*
Anna got	*Anna gat*
you forgot	*thou forgattest* (singular), *ye forgat* (plural)

A couple of other verbs revert to an older form, ending in *-en,* when used with forms of "have":

he has helped	*he hath holpen*
we have held	*we have holden*

And that's all you need to know about verbs in the BCP!

Simpler than you thought, isn't it?

B. A key to pronunciation of Latin terms

As we noted in Chapter 1, canticles are called by their ancient Latin names in the BCP. However, usually you will hear them pronounced in an Anglicized fashion, like this:

Benedicite:	Be-ne-DICE-i-tee
Benedictus:	Be-ne-DICT-us
Cantate Domino:	Can-TAH-tay DO-mi-no
Jubilate:	Ju-bi-LAH-tee
Magnificat:	Mag-NIFF-i-cat
Nunc Dimittis:	Nunc Di-MITT-is
Surge, Illuminare:	SUR-gay il-lu-mi-NAH-ray
Te Deum:	Tee DEE-um
Venite:	Ve-NITE-ee

Psalms also have Latin subtitles, which are their first few words in Latin. But you will hardly ever need to say those, since psalms are almost always referred to by number.

C. A glossary of unusual words found in the BCP

Some of the words listed below are still in use today, but just don't come up in everyday conversation. Others have more than one meaning, or have fallen out of regular use, or have changed their meaning. In the case of words with more than one meaning, this glossary lists the one that is usually meant in the Prayer Book.

A   *abase:* humble, humiliate
abhor: detest, regard with disgust
abide: remain, continue, await
abject: despicable, degraded
abode: dwelling place, home
abominable: detestable, loathsome
abound: be plentiful
abroad: over a wide area, in different directions
absolution: declaration of forgiveness of sins given by a priest
absolve: set free from blame, forgive from sin
abstain: refrain from indulging in
accession: succession to the throne (of a monarch)
accord: agreement, consent
accursed: lying under a curse
adder: small venomous snake
admonish: advise gently, warn
admonition: gentle warning
ado: fuss
adorn: add beauty to, ornament
adversary: opponent, enemy
adversity: misfortune
advocate: person who pleads for another
affection: mental state
afflict: distress with physical or mental suffering
affliction: physical or mental distress, especially pain or illness
affrighted: frightened
afore: before, previously
aforesaid: previously mentioned, said before
aforetime: in earlier times
agreeable: in agreement with

ail: trouble, afflict

alms: charitable donations of money or food given to the poor

almighty: all-powerful

Alpha: beginning (first letter of the Greek alphabet)

amazed: overwhelmed, distressed

amend: improve, correct

amendment: improvement, correction

amid: in the midst of

amiss: wrong, out of place

Anabaptist: type of Protestant, holding among other things that baptism
should only be administered to believing adults

anew: again, in a different way

an-hungred: hungry

anoint: set apart, usually by application of holy oil

anthem: musical setting of sacred words

apparel: clothing

appease: calm, quieten

appertain: belong as a right

aright: rightly

ark: chest or box

array: dress, display

ascribe: attribute, impute

askance: sideways, disapprovingly

assent: consent, agreement

asunder: apart

athirst: thirsty

atonement: reconciliation of God and humanity through Christ's sacrifice

attain: arrive at, reach

aught: anything

avail: help, benefit

B *bade:* commanded, invited, called (past tense of "bid")

banish: expel

banns: announcement of an intended marriage that allows time for any
serious objections

beckon: summon by gesture, wave

become: be fitting, be appropriate

befall: happen (to)

befell: happened (to) (past tense of "befall")

befit: be fitted, appropriate for

begotten: procreated, sprung from

beheld: saw, looked (at) (past tense of "behold")

behold: see, look (at)

benediction: blessing

bequeath: hand down, transmit

beseech: plead earnestly

beset: attack persistently, surround or hem in

besiege: lay siege to

besought: pleaded earnestly, entreated (past tense of "beseech")

bestow: confer

betimes: early, in good time

betwixt: between

bewail: lament, mourn for

bewray: reveal

bid: command, invite, call

bidden: invited, called

bidding: calling, inviting, commanding

bier: moveable frame on which a corpse is taken to a grave

blaspheme: speak irreverently (about)

blasphemy: irreverent speech

bliss: perfect joy, happiness

bounden: obligatory mandatory

bountiful: generous, plentiful, ample

brawler: quarrelsome person

brawn: muscle, meat

breach: break, gap

brethren: brothers and sisters, fellow members

brimstone: sulphur

buckler: small round shield

buffet: blow of the hand or fist; to strike

bullock: bull

bulwark: defensive wall, rampart

busybody: mischief-maker, gossip

by-word: proverb, notable example

C *calamity:* disaster

canonical: in accordance with the canons (laws) of the church

carcase: carcass, dead body

carnal: bodily, worldly
cassia: variety of cinnamon
cast: throw
castaway: lost, rejected, an outcast
catechism: summary of the Christian faith in the form of questions and answers
catechist: a teacher who asks questions from the catechism
catechize: instruct by means of question and answer
catholic: universal
cavil: trivial objection
celestial: heavenly
certify: assure, attest
chaff: dried husks separated from seed
chancel: section of church near the altar, sometimes separated from the
   main body of the church by steps or a screen
charge: command, obligation
chasten: punish, subdue
chastise: reprimand severely, punish
cherubim: second highest order of angels
chiding: scolding, rebuking
christen: baptize and name
circumspect: wary, cautious
citadel: fortress
cleave: adhere, stick fast
cloke: cloak, hide
cloven: split, divided
comfortable: comforting, bringing comfort
commend: entrust, commit
commendation: act of commending
commendatory: commending, entrusting
commit: entrust
committal: burial of a dead body
commodious: convenient
commune: consult secretly
communion: fellowship, sharing
compass: hem in, surround
compassed: hemmed in with, surrounded by
concord: agreement, harmony
concupiscence: sexual desire
coney: small rabbit-like animal of the Middle East

confound: confuse, defeat

confute: prove to be in error

congruity: equivalence, conformity

consanguinity: blood relationship

consecrate: make or declare holy

consecration: separation of a thing or person for a divine purpose, ordination of a bishop

consolation: act or state of being consoled or comforted

console: comfort in grief

consummation: completion, perfection

contend: strive

contrite: repentant, crushed by sense of sin

convenient: suitable

conversation: self-conduct in company of others

corruptible: transient, perishable

corruption: decay, deterioration, decomposition of a corpse

countenance: face

covet: desire wrongfully

covetous: greedy

craft: cunning, deceit

craftiness: deceitfulness

creature: created thing

credence: belief

criminous: criminally minded

cry: shout

cubit: ancient unit of measure, approximately the length of a forearm

cunning: artful; skilled in deceit

curate: pastor; priest acting as assistant to a rector

cure: spiritual charge

D *dearth:* scarcity, lack

deck: adorn, array

defile: make unclean, desecrate, pollute

defilement: uncleanness, pollution

degree: social status

denunciation: speaking against

deride: laugh at, treat with scorn

derision: ridicule, mockery

desirous: wishing, wanting

desolate: ruined, devastated
despise: look down upon, hold in contempt
despiteful: malicious, spiteful
destitute: impoverished, without food or shelter
device: plan, scheme
devise: plan, invent
devour: eat ravenously
devout: sincerely religious
diligence: industriousness, persistent effort
diligent: steady, industrious, attentive
disaffected: discontented, disloyal
disciple: follower of Jesus, especially one of the twelve apostles
discomfit: thwart, baffle
discord: disagreement, strife
discretion: discernment, ability to judge what is right
dispenser: distributor, one who gives out
dispose: make willing, incline
disquiet: worry, trouble
disquietude: uneasiness, anxiety
dissemble: conceal one's motives, act hypocritically
dissimulation: the act of dissembling
divers: various, several, different
doctrine: teaching
double-minded: hypocritical, inconsistent
draught: something drawn out (e.g. a net for fish, or liquid for drinking)
dropsy: disease in which fluid collects in body tissues
dross: scum separated from metals in melting
due: fitting, proper
duly: properly
dwell: live
dwelt: lived

E *earnest:* token or foretaste
earnestly: seriously
ecclesiastical: belonging to the church
edification: enlightenment, improvement by instruction
edify: teach, improve by instruction, enlighten
effectual: effective, actual
effusion: outpouring, shedding

elect: chosen

election: state of having been chosen by God

Ember Day: traditional days of fasting and prayer, especially for ordination candidates

emolument: fee, payment

endeavour: try earnestly, earnest undertaking

endow: enrich, invest

endue: provide, clothe

enkindle: inflame, cause to blaze up

enlighten: shed light upon

enmity: hostility, hatred

ensue: follow

entreat: treat, plead earnestly

equity: justice, fairness

err: go astray, make mistakes

erroneous: incorrect, wrong

eschew: avoid, shun

espouse: become engaged to be married to

espoused: betrothed, engaged to be married

estate: condition or state in life

esteem: value, regard

estimation: opinion of worth, esteem

eventide: evening

ewe: female sheep

exalt: lift up, praise highly

excellency: pre-eminence

excommunicate: cut off from communion with the Church

execute: carry out, perform

exhort: urge, advise earnestly

exhortation: an urging or giving of earnest advice

exigency: urgent need, demand

expedient: suitable, advantageous

expound: explain, interpret

express: exact, explicit

expressly: exactly

F *fable:* invented story, not founded on fact

factious: causing dissensions or factions

fain: willingly, gladly

falsehood: false or untrue thing
fashion: form, shape
fatling: calf or lamb fattened for slaughter
feign: pretend
felicity: happiness
fervent: intense, glowing
fetter: shackle
fie: exclamation of disgust or outrage
firmament: arch of the sky, expanse of heavens
firstling: first born of a season
fit: suitable; make suitable or fitted
flee: run away (from)
fleeting: brief, transitory
flint: hard stone made of silica
flourish: thrive, prosper
fodder: dried hay or straw for cattle
foe: enemy, adversary
fold: enclosure where sheep are kept
folly: foolishness
fond: foolish
forasmuch: because, since
forbear: hold back from, bear with
forefathers: ancestors
forestall: anticipate
forsake: abandon, leave behind
forsook: abandoned, left behind (past tense of "forsake")
forth: forward
forthwith: immediately, without delay
fourscore: eighty (four times twenty)
fowl: bird
fowler: hunter of wildfowl
frailty: weakness
fret: worry, gnaw
frivolous: silly, trivial
froward: perverse, ungovernable
fulfill: satisfy, complete
fuller: one who cleanses and thickens cloth
furlong: an eighth of a mile (220 yards)

G *gainsay:* deny, contradict
gainsayer: one who contradicts or opposes
gape: stare at with open mouth
garner: storehouse, granary
gat: got
gaze: look intently
ghostly: spiritual
gird: fasten with a belt; prepare for action
girdle: belt or cord worn around the waist.
gnash: grind
godliness: devotion to God, piety
godly: pious, devout
grace: divine strengthening and inspiration
graft: implant
grafted: implanted, transplanted
grave: serious
graven: carved (*graven image:* idol)
gravity: seriousness
grievous: severe, causing grief
gross: heavy
guile: deceitful behaviour, treachery

H *hail:* an expression of greeting
hallow: declare holy, make holy
halt: lame, crippled
handmaid: female servant
hart: male deer
havoc: destruction, confusion
hearken: listen
heartily: from the heart
hearty: from the heart
heathen: pagan(s)
heaviness: sorrow
heavy: dejected, sorrowful
heed: take notice of, pay attention to
heifer: young female calf
heinous: utterly odious, atrocious
hence: from this place, from now on
henceforth: from this time onward

hereafter: from now on, after this
hereby: by this (means)
herein: in this (matter)
heresy: false belief or false teaching
heretofore: before this time
hereunto: to this place
hewn: chopped, carved
hid: hidden
Hierome: Greek name of St. Jerome (*c.* 342–420)
hind: female deer
hinder: prevent, obstruct
hindrance: obstruction
hireling: hired servant
hither: to this place
hitherto: until this time
hoar-frost: fine needle-like frost deposited in clear still weather
holden: held (back)
holpen: helped
homily: sermon
Hosanna: "Praise God!" in Aramaic
host: army
hosts: armies
howbeit: nevertheless
humour: state of mind, inclination
hundred-fold: one hundred times
husbandman: farmer
hyssop: small bushy aromatic plant

I   *idolater:* worshipper of idols
ill: harmful, evil
illumine: make bright
immaculate: pure, spotless
immortal: lasting forever
impart: give a share of
impediment: hindrance, obstruction,
impiety: lack of reverence
implore: beg earnestly, entreat
importunity: persistence
imposition: laying on, application

impotent: powerless, helpless
impute: ascribe, attribute
inasmuch (as): since, to the extent (that)
incorruptible: not susceptible to decay, everlasting
incorruption: absence of decay
incumbency: office, tenure
incumbent: rector, one who has charge of a parish
indifferent: neutral
induct: install
inestimable: immeasurable
infirm: physically weak
infirmity: weakness
ingendered: engendered, brought about
iniquity: wickedness, unrighteousness
injunction: authoritative ruling
innocency: innocence
innumerable: uncountable
inordinate: excessive
insomuch: to such an extent
instant: prepared, persistent
institution: establishment, introduction
insurrection: rebellion
intercession: prayer on behalf of another
intimate: make known
invocation: calling upon
irreprehensible: irreproachable, unblameable
issue: outcome, outflow

J   *jest:* joke, jeer
Jewry: the Jewish people
justification: vindication
justify: vindicate

K   *kindly:* pleasant
kindred: relatives, family

L   *lack:* suffer want of, be in need of
laden: burdened
lasciviousness: inappropriate sexual desire

latchet: lace for fastening shoe
laud: praise
laudable: praiseworthy
laver: washing basin
leaven: yeast, substance added to dough to make it rise
let: obstruction, hindrance; obstructed, hindered
Leviathan: a sea monster
licentiousness: lawlessness
lighten: shed light on
liken: compare, represent as similar
list: desire, choose
liturgy: set form of public worship
lo: look!
loin: back of the waist
long-suffering: bearing provocation patiently
lowliness: humility, low estate
lowly: humble, modest
lucre: financial profit, gain
lurk: hide, especially for sinister purposes
lusty: strong, vigorous

M *magistrate:* legal authority
magnify: glorify, render honour to
malefactor: criminal, evildoer
malice: evil will towards another person
mammon: wealth, riches
manfully: bravely, resolutely
manifest: clearly shown or displayed
manifold: many and various
mankind: the human race
mark: notice, pay attention to
meat: food
meek: humble, gentle
meet: suitable, proper
mete: apportion, measure out
Metropolitan: chief bishop in a church province
minded: disposed, inclined,
mindful: conscious, keeping in mind
minished: diminished

minstrel: singer or musician
mire: bog, muck
mirth: merriment, laughter
miscarry: fail, be unsuccessful
mischief: harm, injury
misconstruction: wrong interpretation
misdeed: evil deed, wrongdoing
misdoing: misdeed
miserable: wretchedly unhappy, pitiable
misfortune: bad luck
mock: ridicule, deceive
molten: melted, made of melted metal
monition: warning
morrow: the following day
morsel: small piece, fragment
mortal: ending in death
mortify: bring into subjection by self-discipline
mote: speck (of dust)
multitude: crowd, large number
muse: ponder, reflect
myrrh: resin used in perfume, incense and medicine

N *nativity:* birth
nay: no, rather
nethermost: deepest
newfangleness: unnecessary and objectionable novelty
noisome: harmful, evil-smelling
notorious: unfavourably well-known
notwithstanding: nevertheless, in spite of
nought: nothing
novice: beginner

O *oblation:* offering
octave: period of eight days after and including a church festival; the
   eighth day of this period
office: authorized position; set form of worship
offspring: children, descendants
oft: often
Omega: end (last letter of the Greek alphabet)

omnipotent: all-powerful
oracle: prophet, prophecy
ordain: decree, appoint
orders: appointed position(s) of service in the Church
ordinance: decree
ordinary: bishop or archbishop
outcast: rejected, cast out from the community

P   *palsied:* paralyzed
palsy: paralysis with involuntary tremours
partake: take part in, share in
paschal: belonging to Easter or the Jewish Passover
passion: Christ's suffering on the cross before his death
pate: head
pavilion: tent, decorative building
peculiar: special; belonging (to God)
peevish: spiteful
Pelagian: one who believes man can take the initial steps towards salvation by his own efforts apart from divine grace
penance: act of confessing one's sins to a priest, accepting discipline and receiving absolution
penitence: repentance
penitent: repentant
peradventure: perhaps
perceive: observe, understand
peril: extreme danger
perilous: dangerous
perish: die, suffer destruction
perpetual: continual, everlasting
(in) perpetuity: forever
perplexity: bewilderment
pertain: relate, belong
perverse: persistent in error, wayward, rebellious
pestilence: epidemic disease
piety: devotion to God, reverence of God
pinion: flight feather of a bird's wing
pinnacle: top, peak
pious: devout, reverent
pitiful: deserving or arousing pity; full of pity, compassionate

plague: contagious disease, affliction
plat: weave, braid
plead: appeal, advocate
plenteous: plentiful
plenteousness: plenty
pluck: pull out
pollution: contamination, defilement
pomp: splendour; vainglory
ponder: consider, think over
posterity: succeeding generations, descendents
potsherd: piece of broken pottery
precept: command, moral instruction
premonish: forewarn
prerogative: particular right, privilege
prescribe: lay down, impose
presume: venture, be bold enough
presumptuous: unduly or overbearingly confident
prevail: gain mastery, persuade
prevent: go before
prey: animal hunted by another animal for food
primitive: early, ancient, original
privily: secretly, privately
privy: sharing in the secret of; hidden, secret
procure: obtain, bring about
profane: irreverent, non-religious; to violate or pollute
profess: affirm, state openly
profession: declaration of belief
profitable: beneficial, helpful
pronounce: proclaim
property: characteristic trait or quality
prophesy: foretell (an event); explain the Scriptures
propitiation: atonement, reparation
proselyte: convert
prosper: make successful
prove: test
providence: protective care
provocation: incitement to anger
provoke: incite to anger
prudence: discretion, good judgement

publican: tax collector
publish: make publicly known
purgatory: in Roman Catholic belief, place of punishment and purification from sin after death
purge: purify away
purpose: intend, intent

Q *quick:* living
quicken: rouse, revive
quiver: case for holding arrows

R *rail:* speak abusively
raiment: clothing
ramping: raging, threatening
ravening: plundering, devouring, prowling
ravish: carry off by force
reap: harvest, gather (crops) in
reasonable: proper, rightful
rebuke: reprove, reprimand
reckon: count
recompense: reward
redress: remedy, rectify
reel: swing
refrain: hold back, put restraint upon
refuge: shelter from danger
regenerate: spiritually born again
regeneration: being born again
reliques: part of holy person's body or belongings kept after death as objects of reverence
remiss: lax, negligent
remission: cancelling (of a debt or penalty); pardon
remit: pardon
rend: tear
render: give, pay
renounce: repudiate, forsake
rent: tore, torn
repeal: revoke, annul, rescind
repent: think upon with regret; resolve not to continue (wrongdoing)
repentance: act of repentance; forsaking of sin

repose: rest
reproach: rebuke, blame
reprobate: hardened in sin
reproof: rebuke
reprove: rebuke, blame, scold
repugnant: incompatible, contrary
requisite: required
restitution: compensation, restoration
reverend: worthy of honour or respect
revile: criticize abusively
righteous: virtuous, holding to what is right
righteousness: goodness, virtue
rite: religious ceremony
rochet: surplice-like vestment worn by a bishop
Rogation: three days of solemn prayer before Ascension Day
Romish: Roman Catholic
rubric: directions explaining the conduct of a church service
rude: simple, uneducated

S *sackcloth:* coarse cloth worn as a penance or in mourning
sacrifice: holy offering
saint: believer in Christ, holy person
salutation: greeting
salute: greet
sanctify: consecrate, make holy, set apart
sanctuary: holy place
scarceness: insufficiency, lack
schism: division within the church
school-author: member of a Roman Catholic school of thought known as
   Scholasticism
scoff: mock, taunt
score: twenty
scorn: contempt, hold in contempt
scornful: contemptuous
scourge: whip
scrip: pilgrim's satchel or bag
sedition: plotting or inciting of rebellion
seed: offspring, descendants
seek: look for, search for

seemly: appropriate
sensible: aware
sepulchre: tomb made of stone
seraphim: highest order of angels.
serpent: large snake
seven-fold: seven times, consisting of seven parts
sheaves: bundles of grain tied up after reaping
shod: wearing shoes
shrink: recoil, flinch
shun: avoid; keep clear of
siege: prolonged attack on a fortified place
signification: meaning
slain: killed
slander: false and malicious report about another person
slanderous: speaking slander
slay: kill
sleight: cunning, deception
slew: killed
slipt: slipped
slothful: lazy
slumber: sleep
smite: strike
smitten: stricken, struck
smote: struck (past tense of "smite")
snare: trap
sober: temperate, self-controlled
soil: make dirty
sojourner: temporary resident
solemnization: formal celebration
sore: grievously, severely
sought: looked for, searched for (past tense of "seek")
sow: scatter seed on soil
spare: restrain oneself from punishing or harming
spikenard: costly perfumed ointment
spoil: plunder
stablish: establish
station: position in life
statute: law
stave: staff

stayed: stopped, fixed

stedfast: steadfast, constant, unwavering

stoop: bend forward

stout: brave, resolute

straightway: immediately, at once

striker: violent person

stripe: cut of a whip

strive: try hard, struggle, contend

striving: struggling

stronghold: fortified place

subsist: exist

succour: help, rescue

suckling: unweaned (child or animal)

suffer: allow, permit

suffice: be sufficient

suffrage: short petition

sunder: separate, sever

sundry: various, several

superscription: an inscription over or on a thing

superstition: misdirected reverence

superstitious: holding to superstitions

supplication: humble request

surcease: cease

surety: guarantor, sponsor

swaddling (clothes): narrow lengths of bandage wrapped around a
   newborn child to restrict its movements and quieten it

sworn: having taken an oath, bound by an oath

synod: decision-making church council attended by delegated clergy and laity

T *tabernacle:* tent, sanctuary

talent: ancient unit of weight (thought to be about 26 kg.) of silver or gold

tare: a weed resembling wheat when young

tarry: pause, wait

temperance: moderation, self-restraint

tempest: windy storm

temporal: belonging to this life, worldly

tempt: entice a person to do wrong, put to the test

tender: offer

thence: from that place

thenceforth: from that time on
thereafter: after that
thereby: by that means, as a result of that
therefor: for that purpose
therefrom: from that, from it
therein: in or into that place; in that respect
thereof: of that, of it
thereon: on that, on it
thereto: to that, to it
thereunto: to that, to it
thither: to or towards that place
threefold: three times; consisting of three parts
threescore: sixty (three times twenty)
thrice: three times
throng: crowd
thrust: stab
tidings: news
timbrel: type of tambourine
token: sign, evidence
toll: ring a bell with slow, uniform strokes
tongue: language
transgress: contravene, violate
transgression: violation of law or commandment
transitory: passing, fleeting
travail: labour
tread: press or crush with the feet
treatise: written explanatory work
trespass: offence, wrongdoing
tribulation: great trouble or suffering
tribute: payment to another as a sign of submission
trodden: crushed with the feet
troth: faith, loyalty
troublesome: causing trouble
troublous: trouble-filled
trump: blast of a trumpet
try: test
tumult: uproar, riot
tush: expression of scorn
twain: two

tyrannous: cruel, oppressive
tyrant: person exercising power cruelly

U *unawares:* inadvertently, without anyone knowing
unction: anointing (*extreme unction:* anointing of one near death)
undefiled: pure
unfeigned: genuine, sincere
unfeignedly: genuinely, sincerely, truly
ungodly: wicked, profane
unhallowed: not holy
unrighteousness: wickedness
unruly: disorderly, hard to control
unsatiable: insatiable, impossible to satisfy
unsearchable: mysterious, unfathomable
unseemly: unbecoming, inappropriate
unspeakable: indescribable
unwavering: steady, unfaltering
upbraid: reproach
upright: righteous, honourable, honest
usurp: seize unlawfully
usury: lending money at interest
us-ward: towards us
utter: speak, emit a sound
utterance: power of speech, spoken word
uttermost: remotest, utmost

V *vain:* empty, meaningless (*in vain:* insincerely, without meaning)
vainglory: boastful pride, conceit
vainly: emptily, meaninglessly
vanity: futility, emptiness
vanquish: conquer
vaunt: boast, brag
verily: truly
verity: truth
very: true, genuine
vessel: container, receptacle
vesture: set of garments, covering
vex: irritate, trouble
vial: small glass bottle

viciousness: evil, vice
victuals: food, provisions
vigil: watch kept at night
vigilant: watchful, cautious
virtue: excellence, goodness, strength
vocation: calling
vouchsafe: grant, give

W *wantonly:* irresponsibly, arbitrarily
warrant: written authority
wax: grow, become
waxen: grown, become
whatsoever: whatever
whelp: pup, young animal
whence: from what place
whensoever: whenever
whereas: in contrast with, in comparison with (which)
whereby: by means of which
wherefore: why, on account of which
wherein: in which, in what place or respect
whereinsoever: in whatever
whereof: of which or whom; of what
wheresoever: wherever
whereunto: to which; to what
wherewith: with which, by means of which
wherewithal: with which
whet: sharpen
whither: to what place, result or end, to which
whithersoever: to any place, to which, to wherever
whosesoever: possessive of "whoever"
whoso: who ever
whosoever: whoever
wile: trick, deceit
wiliness: trickery, cunning deceit
wink (at): shut one's eyes to
wise: way, manner
wist: knew
wit: mind, intelligence
withal: as well

without: outside
woe: bitter grief, trouble
wondrous: wonderful
wont: accustomed
wonted: accustomed, usual
wrath: anger, indignation
Writ: Scripture
wroth: angry
wrought: worked, made

Y *yea:* yes, indeed

Z *zeal:* earnestness, fervour

Endnotes

1. C.S. Lewis, *Letters to Malcolm, Chiefly on Prayer.* Geoffrey Bles, London (1964), p. 12.

2. J.I. Packer, *Dr. J.I. Packer's Commentary on the Montreal Declaration of Anglican Essentials.* Essentials, Halifax (1996), p. 49.

3. David Mills, Advent issue, *Anglican Digest,* 1995. Adapted.

4. As quoted in E. H. Peterson, *Answering God: The Psalms as Tools for Prayer.* Harper Collins, San Francisco (1989), p. 36.

5. Anne Lamott, *Travelling Mercies: Some Thoughts on Faith.* Pantheon, New York (1999), p. 82.

6. C.S. Lewis, op. cit., pp. 108–9.

7. C.S. Lewis, *Mere Christianity.* Macmillan, New York (1952), p. 142–143.

8. C.S. Lewis, *The Efficacy of Prayer,* reprinted from *Atlantic Monthly* (1958) by Forward Movement Publications Cincinnati, Ohio, p. 4.

9. Unpublished funeral sermon by Chris King, rector of Little Trinity Anglican Church, Toronto, preached at the funeral of Bruce Black on June 20, 1999.

10. Anthony Burton, Bishop of Saskatchewan, in his cover endorsement of *The Collects of Thomas Cranmer* by C. Frederick Barbee and Paul F. M. Zahl, Wm. B. Eerdmans Publishing Co., Grand Rapids, Michigan (1999).

11. Brother Lawrence, *The Practice of the Presence of God: Being Conversations and Letters of Nicholas Herman of Lorraine,* Spire Books, Fleming H. Revell Co., New Jersey, (1958), Reprint 1973, p. 54.

12. Ibid., pp. 39, 29.

13. Jacob Astley, quoted in *The Oxford Book of Prayer,* Oxford University Press, Oxford (1985).

14. Helmut Thielicke, *The Prayer That Spans the World: Sermons on the Lord's Prayer* (1953), English translation, John W. Doberstein, James Clarke & Co. Ltd., Cambridge (1965).

15. Dietrich Bonhoeffer, *Psalms: The Prayer Book of the Bible,* Augsburg Publishing House, Minneapolis (1970), pp. 9–12.

16. E.H.Peterson, *Answering God: The Psalms as Tools for Prayer,* Harper Collins, San Francisco (1989), pp. 99–103 for an in depth treatment of this concept.

17. Miroslav Volf, *Exclusion and Embrace,* as quoted in *The Bible Jesus Read* by Philip Yancey, p. 138. Zondervan Publishing House, Grand Rapids, Michigan (1999).

18. Dietrich Bonhoeffer, *Psalms: The Prayer Book of the Bible,* pp. 57-58, Augsburg Publishing House, Minneapolis, (1970).

19. Ibid., p. 59.

20. John Stott, *The Authority of the Bible,* InterVarsity Press booklet (1974), pp. 29–30. Originated as an address given at the Urbana 73 InterVarsity Missionary Convention.

21. Philip Yancey, *The Bible Jesus Read,* Zondervan Publishing House, Grand Rapids, Michigan (1999). p. 25.

22. John Stott, op. cit., p. 29.

23. Alister McGrath, *I Believe: Understanding and Applying the Apostles' Creed,* Zondervan Publishing Company, Grand Rapids, Michigan (1991).

24. Robert Crouse, in *The Lord is Nigh: The Theology and Practice of Prayer,* Sparrow Publishing (1997), p. 78. Papers from the Western Theological Conference, held by the Okanagan Branch of the Prayer Book Society of Canada, Kelowna, B.C., August 8-11, 1995.

25. St. Augustine, *Confessions,* Book 10, Chapter 27 (397–98 AD).

26 • The Talmud (1st–6th cent. AD) Rabbinical writings.
   • St. Cyprian (*c.* 200–258 AD) Bishop of Carthage and martyr.
   • Willian McGill, "Prayer Unceasing", *Living Church,* 28 September, 1986.
   • Martin Buber (1878–1965) *Eclipse of God: Studies in the Relation between Religion and Philosophy,* p. 8, 1952.
   • Abraham Joshua Herschel (1907–1972) *Man's Quest for God: Studies in Prayer and Symbolism,* p. 1, 1954.
   • Eugene H. Peterson, *Answering God: The Psalms as Tools for Prayer,* p. 113, Harper San Franciso, (1989).
   • Robert Crouse, op. cit., p. 77.
   • J.I. Packer, as confirmed in conversation on March 24, 2003.
   • Anthony Burton, Bishop of Saskatchewan, *Incourage,* Volume 13, Number 3, 2000, p. 5. Publication of Barnabas Anglican Ministries.
   • Brother Lawrence, op. cit., p. 48.
   • Mother Teresa of Calcutta (1910–1997), quoted in *The Complete Idiot's Guide to Prayer,* Mark Galli and James S. Bell, Jr., Alpha Books, MacMillan, Indianapolis, (1999), p. 65.
   • St. Augustine, *Confessions,* Book 1, Chapter 1 (397–98 AD).